PENGUIN BOOKS

playtime

Elspeth Richards is a teacher, mother of three adult children and grandparent, with over 40 years' experience working with young children. She has taught in schools in the United States, the United Kingdom and Australia. She was a professional pianist and taught piano for many years. She lives in Sydney.

Fiona Richards qualified as a lawyer in Sydney and received her MBA from the IE Business School in Madrid. She has spent the last 12 years in London and Hong Kong, working in news publishing and television. With her husband and two young sons, she has recently returned to Sydney.

ELSPETH & FIONA RICHARDS

play
time

Activities for little children
that can make a big difference

PENGUIN BOOKS

PENGUIN BOOKS

Published by the Penguin Group
Penguin Group (Australia)
250 Camberwell Road, Camberwell, Victoria 3124, Australia
(a division of Pearson Australia Group Pty Ltd)
Penguin Group (USA) Inc.
375 Hudson Street, New York, New York 10014, USA
Penguin Group (Canada)
90 Eglinton Avenue East, Suite 700, Toronto, Canada ON M4P 2Y3
(a division of Pearson Penguin Canada Inc.)
Penguin Books Ltd
80 Strand, London WC2R 0RL, England
Penguin Ireland
25 St Stephen's Green, Dublin 2, Ireland
(a division of Penguin Books Ltd)
Penguin Books India Pvt Ltd
11 Community Centre, Panchsheel Park, New Delhi – 110 017, India
Penguin Group (NZ)
67 Apollo Drive, Rosedale, North Shore 0632, New Zealand
(a division of Pearson New Zealand Ltd)
Penguin Books (South Africa) (Pty) Ltd
24 Sturdee Avenue, Rosebank, Johannesburg 2196, South Africa

Penguin Books Ltd, Registered Offices: 80 Strand, London, WC2R 0RL, England

First published by Penguin Group (Australia), 2009

10 9 8 7 6 5 4 3 2 1

Text copyright © Elspeth & Fiona Richards 2009

The moral right of the author has been asserted

Design by Elissa Christian © Penguin Group (Australia)
Cover photograph by Julie Renouf
Typeset in 10.5/16 pt Berkeley Oldstyle Medium by Post Pre-press Group, Brisbane, Queensland
Printed and bound in Hong Kong by 1010 Printing International Ltd

National Library of Australia
Cataloguing-in-Publication data:

Richards, Elspeth.
Playtime : activities for little children that can make a big difference / Elspeth & Fiona Richards.
9780143007869 (pbk.)
Bibliography.
Play.
Games.
Learning.
Richards, Fiona.

649.5

penguin.com.au

Tell me and I will forget,
show me and I might remember,
involve me and I will understand

Old Chinese saying

Contents

Preface

SHORTLY AFTER my husband and I moved to Hong Kong with our
first child, then one year old, I found myself at a bit of a loss. Having
spent most of my son's first year working full-time in London, it was a
shock to suddenly find myself in his company all of the time. I realised
I didn't really know him – I didn't understand much of his behaviour,
his likes and dislikes, his mood changes, his attempts at speech. And
he was changing so fast. How should I play with him, talk to him, help
him to learn? What if I went back to work again – would I feel so out of
touch with him once more? I tried to get help from books and Internet
sources, and to enlist the support of extended family – but they were
over 7000 kilometres away. In desperation, I asked my mother, Elspeth,
to start writing down some of the play ideas she has used as a teacher of
so many different children – ideas that seemed so effortless and natural
to her after many years of practice. Over the next two years, we kept
discussing different ideas and the responses of my son, his cousins and
friends, and my mother kept writing it all down. She discovered that
it's not necessarily easy to write about things that come to you quite
naturally; you don't really think about it – you just do it, say it. But she

persisted and the results appear in Chapter 10.

Having forced ourselves to think more deeply about play in early childhood, we felt we were just scratching the surface of an immense and fascinating topic. There was so much for parents to learn about the inherent characteristics of a young child, the value of so many forms of play and how to make the most of these precious early years. This prompted us to try to organise various play ideas in a simple and useful way for parents. My interest in the topic was further fuelled by my son attending a Montessori preschool in Hong Kong. Observing well-trained early-learning educators in this environment made me want to understand more about the Montessori philosophy. A number of ideas in this book have been inspired by Dr Montessori's writings and the learning approach adopted by my son's preschool.

Writing this book has brought to mind many wonderful people who interact so well with children. It's been a pleasure to pause and reflect on this. My mother, for example, still recalls the kindness shown to her then two-year-old son by the headmaster at our local primary school. Big school. Busy man. But on the occasions my mother would visit the school office with her son, he would come out to greet them and stick a little notice to his door. It simply said 'GONE FISHING'. He would pick up the little boy and take him out to inspect the concrete mixer and the cranes on the school building site, and discuss them with him. My brother couldn't have been happier in his company. As parents, we always remember people who make time to engage with our children – even if it is just for a minute or two. It doesn't require much effort at all once you know how to do it, but the impression it leaves is strongly felt by parents and children alike.

Fiona Richards

Introduction

How MANY BOOKS are out there on the vast topic of early child-hood? How much information can you pull up on the Internet simply by typing in the words 'toddler tantrums', or 'what to buy your three-year-old' or, heaven forbid, 'how to teach your toddler to read'? How many conversations have you had with other parents that have revolved solely around your efforts to toilet-train your child – or, worse, their efforts to toilet-train theirs?

Parents and society alike are very good at talking *about* children. But how good are we at talking *with* children? How comfortable are we getting down on our knees and having a conversation at their level? How inclined to become involved in a little game they want to play, or to suggest one ourselves?

OUR ROLE IN CHILD'S PLAY

As adults we tend to have quite fixed views on what 'play' means. We'll say things like, 'The kids are just playing outside', or 'He's playing with his blocks', but we rarely put ourselves into the equation. We see play as something children do on their own or with their siblings or peers, perhaps because we don't quite understand what they are doing or why they are doing it.

This notion of 'child's play' as something totally free from adult involvement has led to some confusion about one of the most basic aspects of a young child's life. Of course there is an important element of child's play that is a child's territory alone. As adults, we must respect this and be mindful of when children need time to themselves. This becomes even more relevant in the later years of childhood when children hit the playgrounds, socialise more with their peers and develop their own games. But in the very early years, child's play involves something slightly different. What we call 'play' is a young child's natural way of learning, not only by imitating what we say and do, but also by exploring the world about them and testing their own abilities.

Using their senses to guide them, they engage in all kinds of repetitive, self-driven activity to achieve these aims. But young children don't learn through their own play alone. Instinctively, they seek the company of parents and other familiar faces and try to interact with us – time and time again. Your child may show the keenest interest in 'helping' you clean the bath, choose oranges at the shop, bake a cake or do some gardening at home; he'll be thrilled when you take an interest in the snail he has just spotted on the path or involve him in a story or game. He wants your assurance, guidance and conversation. While this can drive us to distraction sometimes and leave us with little time to ourselves, it is a most endearing part of child's play. No one else in the world is as pleased with our company as he is.

Our role in child's play is not restricted to structured or scheduled play activities. Play can become a natural part of everything we do with our child. Whether you are getting him dressed, going for a walk, listening to music or just reading a book together, you can engage in play and discussion with your child – even just for a minute or two. It might seem small, and you will not always feel like it. But through these unforced and regular interactions, you set some crucial foundations – not only for your child's learning, but for a lifelong relationship between you.

LEARNING THROUGH PLAY

Much has been written about the extraordinary instinct of a young child to explore, talk and interact with us. It's at the heart of many early-learning philosophies – among them, Montessori. More recently, it has been summed up by the catchphrase 'learning through play'. If you haven't yet come across this phrase in other material, you soon will. It's used constantly by early-childhood educators and commentators, and by many preschools and early-learning centres.

Despite its almost universal acceptance, the concept of 'learning through play' has made a lot of parents feel uncomfortable. Some of us find it hard to see child's play as anything more than 'just' play. Others might have some understanding of how play and learning go hand in hand, but feel that the business of play (or is it learning?) might best be outsourced rather than practised in the home. With such an abundance of playgroups and commercial activities to choose from, parents can be forgiven for thinking like this. Many of us are short of time as we try to juggle work, family and other competing needs. But we all want the best for our child. So why not hand it over to the experts, we wonder – especially if that's how children 'learn'? There's a muffled chant coming from parents these days: How can I engage in play with my child? What do I say? How long should I play? What do I do if they won't stay and play? Others can do this better, can't they?

Our purpose in writing this book is to help adults work up some skills in this thing called 'play' and to start to see it in a more positive way. Play *is* how children learn (as we'll see throughout this book), but it's also how *we* learn about our children. Armed with some easy ideas, we can start to sense how they are thinking and what might appeal to them at a particular time. Every adult is capable of this but most of us need to learn a few tricks of the trade.

THINKING SMALL

Some people seem instinctively at ease with young children. They simply know what to say and how to play. Children pick up on this immediately and happily hover around such people. Unfortunately, though, child's play does not come naturally to many of us. We are not all wired like Peter Pan, and of course we have forgotten what it is like to be a young child.

 I still recall taking my then five-month-old on his first long-haul flight to see his extended family. The trip was nothing short of a nightmare. So much for being lulled to sleep by the dulcet sounds of the engines; he was distressed from beginning to end – at least, that is my memory of it. On arrival, my mother suggested we sing to him to calm him down. It seemed rather foreign to me, singing to this little child without yet knowing his personality, not knowing for certain if he was happier with Humpty or Handel. Nevertheless, the more we sang the more he seemed comforted by it. →

> It was one of those small but precious parental moments when you finally find something that appeals, peace is re-established and life is wonderful again.

Of course there are times when we don't feel inclined to play, talk or sing, even when the moment calls for it. As we get older and more easily exhausted, it possibly gets more difficult – and yet, many of us are having children at an older age. At other times, we may desperately want to play with our child but have very limited time to do so. As more of us try to juggle work and child care, how do we make the most of short bursts of time with our child in the morning and evening? If we are returning home from work, how do we switch off the work mindset and talk to him? Do we ask him how his day was? No – he is not interested in the past. He's on for the here and now. We need to be prepared to engage with him immediately at his level and think about topics of conversation and activities that might be of interest to him *right now*.

And while we are away from him we are leaving the business of play to others. You may be relying on childcare workers, nannies or other carers to look after your child during the day. Grandparents, too, may be sharing much of the load. But some grandparents have had little to do with young children for 30 years or more. How can you help others enjoy the time they spend with your child? Can you offer more guidance other than to say, 'Please do some counting with him', or 'The puzzles are in there'? Do you really need to buy another 'educational' toy in the hope that it will keep him stimulated while you are away?

TUNING IN TO YOUR CHILD

Every child is different. Each develops a preference for certain types of play in much the same way as we develop preferences for certain playlists on our MP3 player; we might listen to the same one over and over and then, suddenly, switch to something different. Throughout this book we emphasise the importance of seeking out the type of play that most suits your child's personality, mood and moment. Not every activity in this book is going to appeal. And some may not appeal on the first, second or even third tries, but if you leave it for a while and then try again, all of a sudden your child may keep asking for it.

Most of all, our role requires patience. In the very early years it is not always immediately obvious that children have cottoned on to anything that we are telling them. This is the puzzle of their 'absorbent mind', as Dr Montessori explains in her extraordinary book of the same title (see Further Reading, page 193). We know they are absorbing vast amounts of information but we do not know quite what is 'going in' at any particular time or when they will let us know about it. Half the time they don't even look like they are concentrating on what we are saying. This can be quite off-putting for adults, especially those of us used to working in results-driven environments. But their little minds will surprise you. They will have processed words and phrases when you thought they weren't paying attention. They will remember places, actions, rhythms, tunes, expressions, emotions. Rejoice when you do see results but do not be hard on yourself (or your child) when you don't see the immediate effect of your input – just give any activity your best shot and move on.

THINGS MY MOTHER TAUGHT ME

If you are a little daunted by these words, fear not. As I learnt from my mother – someone always at ease with small companions – child's play is not as random as it might first appear. There are some childhood characteristics that are surprisingly universal. If you are fairly new to this game, it does help to know a bit about these.

The following characteristics generally start to become apparent in a child's first year, and, with the right encouragement, will reveal themselves in different ways throughout his early years. Play is so much easier once you understand what children love to do!

A desire to explore

Young children act a little like aliens arriving on this earth on some sort of quest to investigate. Using their senses to guide them, they seek out anything that moves, catches their eye, feels or sounds interesting; and they delight in handling things for the first time.

Encourage this insatiable desire to explore, discover and experiment with plenty of sensory stimuli. We talk about the need for sensory stimuli throughout this book – not least, stimulation for little hands. Hands-on involvement is not just a child's way of learning about the world, remembering what things are and how they work; it's also their way of mastering the many fine hand movements eventually required to write, draw, use a computer and engage in other practical and creative tasks.

Of course they can't touch everything they want to. Safety must always be at the forefront of our minds, especially in these early years. But do let them experiment as much as possible with all kinds of ordinary objects – not just toys – as they explore the world around them.

An ear for language

One of the greatest sources of sensory stimulation for a young child is simply your voice. Your child loves the sound of it more than any other sound and his ears are totally attuned to identifying it. This characteristic is immediately apparent from birth. Turning to the sound of your voice, your baby will watch the movement of your mouth with interest. This encourages you to talk more and so the process of language development begins.

Gradually babies start to imitate what they hear and see. The most extraordinary thing is that, in the early years – and *only* at this time of their lives – learning a language happens naturally. As Montessori recognised, no child tires of learning his mother tongue, however complex that may be. Make the most of your child's remarkable instinct for language by conversing about everything that is going on around him. He *really* wants to know. Just use normal words – there's no need for 'baby talk'. But keep in mind that this little person is learning how to speak, no less, and there are some things you can do to make that easier for him (see Chapter 1).

An ear for music

As with language, a young child's ear is highly receptive to musical sounds. This makes playing music one of the easiest forms of play. Every culture loves music of some form or another. And every child responds to music in some way: some love the soothing effects of a bedtime lullaby, some may love to dance or march around the room and some may be quick to drum out a rhythm or make up a little tune. In Chapter 8 we look at different ways to play music with a child – ways to suit the moment as well as your child's musical preferences. Be sure to include music in your repertoire of play activities – its impact in the early years is powerful, positive and potentially long-lasting.

A need to repeat actions

In the early years, you do not need to remind your child that practice makes perfect. Just as a child starts to master language through repetitive use of words and phrases, so he starts to master actions through repetitive activity. This will begin with what seem to us to be the most mundane of actions – putting little plastic barrels inside each other, for example, or replacing a cap on a bottle. But repeating a chosen activity, often for weeks on end, is simply a child's way of getting to grips with one thing. Through this wonderfully instinctive process he begins the enormous preparation required to imitate what we do and to begin to understand the physical world around him. Encourage this by allowing your child to do the same activity again and again if he likes it. There is no need to have a lot of variation if your child is quite happy. If he seeks your company or involvement in these endeavours, just work on the same thing quietly alongside him so he can also observe what you are doing.

A need for order

It's easy to think that a small child's world is a chaotic one. (That's certainly the way they seem to leave the house!) Despite appearances, however, a child's sense of order is remarkably intense in the very early years. This might manifest itself in the strangest of ways.

 I remember my 12-month-old's consternation on the rare occasions when we would shut the door between the kitchen and the general living area. We couldn't fathom his distress the first time it happened and thought he must have injured →

himself. But the problem was simply that he didn't like that door closed. This was not how he normally found it. In his mind, it was completely out of order.

Young children even like to find their toys in order, so that they know where they are and can choose which ones they want to play with. You may notice that if you pack all their toys away together in one big box, they will tend to leave them there. But if you sort out the toys a bit – on a shelf, for example – then it's easier for your child to find his chosen activity. And he often does know *exactly* what he is looking for.

Having fewer toys in the room is a good idea as well. Try rotating toys by packing some away for a month or so. When you bring them out again, they are as good as new to your child. This has the added benefit of reducing clean-up time and keeping the toy bills down.

In Chapter 5 we look at different play ideas that appeal to your child's sense of order: counting things, putting things in order, matching shapes and patterns, and doing puzzles. You will see how you can adapt these ideas as your child gets older. The activities may seem simple; they may only take a minute or two. But, repeated regularly over a child's early years, these little activities set some important foundations – not just for the development of numeracy skills in the longer term, but for so many other skills that rely on a clear and orderly mind.

A love of routine

Knowing the order for the day is also important to a young child. He likes to know what is going to happen next, so talk to him about it.

Routine activities help him to feel secure. In Chapter 1 you will see how you can make the most of this by playing little games with him while he is in the bath or while he is waiting for breakfast. Your child will often respond better at these times, when he's expecting his usual bathtime or breakfast-time activity, rather than if you say to him out of the blue, 'Let's play a game.'

A desire for independence

Young children have a natural urge to get involved in everything they see us doing. This is their way of learning to do things by themselves. Even a one-year-old will be thrilled when you ask him to put on his socks. Of course he won't be able to do it without help, but he might start by moving his socks in the direction of his feet, copying what he has seen you do.

In all your activity with your child, be aware of this basic desire for independence. During routine activities, let him take pride in achieving little tasks. Let him start to put on his clothes, wash and dry his hands and brush his teeth. As he gets older he will love to say, 'I can do it all by myself.' At mealtimes, ask your child to get out his own cup and plate, and to find the butter in the fridge. He will love to pour a drink from his own small jug. Of course there will be spillage sometimes but let him learn how to be careful. Help him to think and work things out for himself.

There are so many little ways in which you can encourage your child to take responsibility. In a number of the games in Chapter 10, for example, we suggest sometimes giving your child the role of instructor and communicating instructions to you, rather than always the other way around. Children love this idea – they think it's a great game!

A love of surprise, fun and drama

Whether you are telling him a story, making up a little game or just searching for a small distraction for your child, make use of the elements of surprise, fun and drama. Like any good actor, one of the simplest ways to do this is to vary your tone of voice or change your facial expression. So you might whisper to your child or speak with a funny accent or look really surprised at something. This technique is particularly important when you are telling him a story, as we explore further in Chapter 2.

If I had to pick one child's game that best captures the elements of surprise, fun and drama, it would be hide-and-seek. Think of how a baby loves you covering your face with your hands and playing 'Boo!' with him. He laughs every time. This fascination with hiding carries on right through the early years – whether it's you hiding, them hiding or you hiding something for them to find. Books cater to this childhood obsession as well, with flaps that lift up to reveal another picture 'hidden' underneath.

It's amusing to watch a child's understanding of hiding develop. At first they think no one can see them when they hide their face. It takes them some time to work out whether they are hiding or you are hiding. As they get older and start playing early games of hide-and-seek, some children will use the same hiding places over and over again. Some love the great sense of anticipation as you walk around trying to find them. Others are not able to stay hidden for long at all. And at what age does a young child understand that if they call out 'I'm ready!', they give away where they are hiding?

A number of the ideas in this book introduce the concept of hiding – whether it's hiding something behind your back, in a bag or under a cloth, going on a treasure hunt, telling a story that involves a missing toy or animal (where is it hiding?) or learning to play hide-and-seek.

A love of make-believe

One of the most delightful forms of children's play takes place when they try to *be* someone else or involve their toys in adult-like activities. This goes beyond their natural impulse to simply imitate things we do (by dressing up in our clothes, sweeping the floor with a small broom or taking their toy dog for a walk in a stroller, for example). Toys come alive for them through this role-play activity and become their fanciful friends.

In Chapter 4 we encourage you to indulge your child in these fantasy worlds: go on that bear hunt, have a tea party for all their soft toys or look after a doll that is sick. Although young children will often engage happily in these games on their own, they will love your involvement sometimes.

HOW TO USE THIS BOOK

In the chapters that follow we explore nine basic forms of play that make the most of what comes naturally to a child. We call these 'play themes' and each has its own symbol:

 play and routine

 reading and storytelling

 letters and words

 role play and make-believe

numbers and order

 hands at work

 sensing and feeling

 music and movement

 exploring and discovering

We look at some of the skills that each theme helps to develop. We suggest ways to incorporate these play themes into your child's day. For those wanting more guidance, Chapter 10 offers step-by-step instructions on how to play some simple games with children aged one to five years. The symbol beside each game indicates which play theme is featured. You will soon see how you can develop the play themes to suit your child's personality and preferences; and how you can adapt play to appeal to children of different ages. For activities to do with babies and ideas for grandparents who live far away from their grandchildren, see Appendixes 1 and 2.

There is no need to follow each chapter of this book in sequence – it is designed so that you can dip in and out. You may, for example, want to know why your toddler loves you talking to his toy rabbit or why your four-year-old constantly wants to dress up – in which case you could turn to Chapter 4. You may just want some guidance on reading to your child: what to read, how to read and whether to read the same bedtime story again and again if he requests it – in which case you could start at Chapter 2.

No doubt you are already practising some of the ideas in this book. But, like any aspect of parenthood, there are things to learn about play, in all its forms. We hope some extra skills will both reassure you about what you are already doing and inspire you to do more.

Age guides

Although age recommendations are given for the games, keep in mind that these are just suggestions. Don't be too concerned about when your child 'should' be doing a particular activity. Unfortunately there is quite a culture of parental anxiety around child development. It's hard to escape those seemingly 'friendly' conversations about what someone else's child is up to without feeling worried that your child is not keeping up. And when so much of what we read about and are encouraged to buy for our children is categorised in terms of developmental stages, it's difficult not to feel preoccupied by these.

Of course it can be reassuring to have some age guidance – particularly for a first child. But too much focus on measurable milestones skews our perspective on our child's development. We fail to see the importance of many small activities in our child's day. We also fail to see how different activities work together to achieve certain goals. Why, for example, do we clap excitedly when our two-year-old kicks a ball but perhaps take less notice when he carefully stands little plastic animals in a row or moulds playdough into some sort of shape? As we'll see in Chapter 6, repetition of this type of activity helps to develop the fine-motor skills involved in eventually being able to write and engage in other amazing handiwork.

Every little activity in these early years is a stepping stone to another. Be happy that your child is learning at his own pace. His instinct to learn through play will manifest itself in so many delightful ways. To flourish, it requires freedom, security, time, an assortment of sensory stimuli – and lots of little interactions with you.

1. Our Daily World

PLAY AND ROUTINE

MOST OF US STRIVE to establish some sort of routine for our child's basic activities during her first year – sleeping, feeding, bathing, playing with toys, going for a walk and so on. Despite what some books may have you believe, it is not easy. Babies take time to settle into a pattern. They seem hungry one minute then not hungry, at peace with their world then quickly distressed by it and unable to feed or get to sleep. They experiment with crying a lot or simply have their own idea of what constitutes a good night's sleep. And that's a 'normal' baby!

Then there is you to consider. If this is your first child you may have become used to being a fairly free agent for many years before having children. Now, you find yourself locked into this little person's so-called routine. 'But what about *my* routine?' you feel like crying. 'What about the eight hours sleep I used to have each night? What about long Sunday breakfasts with the newspaper?' Suddenly your routine is in tatters (as is the newspaper if little hands have half a chance to grab it).

Gradually, however, after much mental and physical adjustment, a new daily routine starts to evolve. It's not something that needs to be followed too rigidly but it does give some sense of order to the day. And it is not only you that gains comfort from this; undertaking the same activity in more or less the same manner and at the same time each day helps your child start to feel secure in the world.

Young children like routine activities simply because they like to know what is happening next.

THE IMPORTANCE OF FEELING SECURE

A sense of security is vital not just for babies but right through early childhood. When a child feels secure she is more receptive to what's going on around her. She is ready to absorb the vast quantities of new information being thrown at her each day. In short, she is ready to learn.

At age four, my son still talked about his routine a lot: 'Tomorrow we will get up, have breakfast, get dressed, brush our teeth, put our shoes on . . . and then we will [go to the museum]'. Although he was excited about doing something different (like going to a museum or visiting friends), he still liked the reassurance that some things about the day would be exactly the same as the previous day. He would also reiterate his routine activities in his play. He enjoyed, for example, putting his toy animals through his routine: 'The raccoons are having breakfast', 'Snail is having a bath', 'Bear is putting on his shoes to go for a walk.'

Think about why a daily bedtime story works such wonders with a young child. She quickly learns that when you sit down to look at a book together you will be with her for at least a short while and giving your full attention to this activity. This puts her at ease and leaves her ready to absorb what's being said and shown to her on the page. By performing the activity on a regular basis and in roughly the same manner each time, you start to create the perfect environment for learning – the more she learns during your reading sessions, the more she wants to learn. The routine of reading books becomes self-reinforcing.

Like the daily bedtime story, other routine activities in your child's day – getting dressed, having a meal, having a bath and so on – provide perfect opportunities for learning through play, and especially for developing language skills. Of course, this takes time. A baby's first bath, for example, is often a traumatic experience for all parties involved. It's hard for first-time parents to imagine performing this activity on a daily basis. But by persisting with it each day – gradually working out how best to hold her, how warm to make the water, how on earth to wash her hair, where to put the towel – your anxieties start to diminish and you even manage to mutter a few words of calm. Soon your baby starts to associate the word 'bath' with a happy and familiar activity. She becomes immensely enthusiastic about the prospect of performing the same little routine that she undertook the day before. Once she is relaxed you can start to show her things – your hands, her hands, her tummy, her feet, a plastic duck, or water pouring out of a jug – and talk about them. You don't need to do or say very much. Happily engaged in a familiar activity, she will respond to things she can see, hear and touch, and start to absorb what you say about them.

Some of the games we suggest playing while getting your child dressed, giving her a bath or undertaking other routine activities (look for the 🕐 symbol in Chapter 10) might seem obvious. But it is surprising how easily we forget to make the most of these times when our child is at ease, engaged in a familiar activity and ready to absorb what we are saying. By recognising the importance of these routine activities to your child and how much she can learn at these brief times, you will start to view them slightly differently. You will feel satisfied by a two-minute 'discussion' with your daughter while getting her dressed in the morning. And you will enjoy focusing on topics other than how much your child is eating at mealtimes. And, no doubt, so will your child.

Don't restrict yourself to the activities we suggest. Think about other routine occurrences in your child's week. Do you take her to the shops? Are you often in the car with her? What things could you talk about at these times?

WHAT TO TALK ABOUT

Throughout their early years children remain largely focused on what is going on in front of them at any moment in time. Past events, let alone nebulous future events, are not within their grasp and tend not to be interesting topics of conversation for them. This is not to say they don't remember things that have happened to them, places they have visited and people they have met, and of course you can talk about those things with them. But they do get very easily distracted by the here and now – they don't sit back and reminisce for long. So they might remember something that happened when they visited a farm two weeks ago but, rather than discussing that too much, they would prefer to get started on building or drawing a farm and talking about that.

For the same reason, you might find it difficult to strike up a discussion with your child about her day at preschool, as much as you would love to know what went on. As far as she is concerned, that event is over and therefore not interesting. She would much prefer to talk to you about the snail she spots on the footpath on the way home. So, talk to her about the snail – what colour it is, what it likes to eat, where it might be going, how slowly it moves, whether it's a 'Max' or a 'Mindy' and what it will do if it rains. This is just the sort of dialogue you might have with her when you are showing her the pictures of a book. And she is thrilled about it.

Of course, we can't always rely on our child to find interesting topics of conversation, like a passing snail. We need to plan things to talk about and find other distractions. And the more subtly we do it, the better. A child will often take more interest in something she has 'found' herself rather than something that is thrust into her hands. This is a way of asserting her independence. But none of this need involve too much work on your part. If you are aware of *when* your child is likely to be the most receptive and *what* kind of activities and topics of conversation will command her attention, the rest is easy. Through playful and appropriate conversation and activity, you can subtly introduce to your child a whole range of words, topics and concepts.

HOW TO TALK

You can start these 'discussions' as early as you like. You may feel a little strange at first, chattering away without much of a reaction from her. Even as she reaches toddler age, you may feel discouraged by her short attention span or lack of eye contact; you may have difficulty understanding her responses (and all the more so if you are trying to engage with someone else's child).

Don't be hard on yourself if it doesn't immediately feel natural and enjoyable to you. But don't give up, either. Soon she will surprise you by repeating what you say and imitating the way you say it. By the age of five, your child will be bursting with things to say, curious about the world and asking you questions about everything.

We always remember those who make an effort to engage with our children – even just for a minute or two. Observe people who do seem at ease with children. What are they doing to capture the child's attention? Here are some simple techniques my mother taught me:

Get on the same level

When talking with a child directly, get down to her level as much as possible. Or, if she's very small, pick her up or take her hand to show her things. She loves to be right near your voice as she learns what's what.

Say it again

When helping your child to communicate, remind yourself what it's like to hear a foreign language. You know how difficult it is to understand someone if they speak too quickly. You just want them to say it again – slowly – then again. Although a young child's ability to learn a language is infinitely better than ours, they also like hearing the same words and phrases again and again – whether as part of a story, rhyme, song or game, or just while going about routine activities.

By repeating words and phrases clearly, your child will not only learn to say exactly what you have just said, but will copy the way you said it as well.

Use simple phrases . . .

. . . but don't be afraid to use big words occasionally, too. Tell her what the word means, use it again and leave it at that for the moment. She may remember it the next time she hears it, or she may not. She may grow to like the sound of a word like 'deciduous'; she may surprise you one day by pointing out a 'pachycephalosaurus'.

Ask questions with two-word choices

This will encourage a two-word response rather than simply a 'Yes' or a 'No'. For example, ask 'Do you want to eat the big apple or the little apple?', 'Do you want to wear your red shirt or your blue shirt?' or 'Do you want your farm book or your penguin book?'

Add some drama

If your child is bored, up to a bit of mischief, or unable to stop crying, a little diverting conversation can be enough to change the mood. For example, you could say, suddenly and with much drama:

Ssshush! LISTEN! What's THAT noise? (You will inevitably hear something – a plane, a train, a siren, water in the washing machine.)

Ssshush! LOOK! Can you see that little bird right up high in the tree?

Play with language

Have fun with word sounds, rhymes, accents and absurdities. Answer your own question with a silly answer then ask her if it is correct. Use actions and facial expressions to demonstrate what a word means. As your child gets older she will love to be asked to 'make a *happy* face' (or a *surprised, sad, angry* face) and will be thrilled if you make one too.

2. Once Upon a Time . . .

READING AND STORYTELLING

When my son was three, my mother used to tell him her version of a fairytale she remembered from her childhood about the Little Red Hen. He loved this story and requested it each time she came to visit. As he got to know the story better he would tell her immediately if she got anything wrong and would remind her of any forgotten details. Why was he so interested in the same tale again and again? And how did he remember it between visits, which were few and far between because we were living overseas? There were no pictures and she used no props except her fingers. It was just the way she told the story that seemed to captivate him. She would always sit on the floor with him, and she used different voices for the different characters, and strong facial expressions to show happiness, sadness and surprise. She →

also involved him in the story by walking her fingers across his hands and feet (to show the Little Red Hen going to visit one of her friends) and asking him to choose which friend the Little Red Hen would visit next. Having had stories read to him regularly since he was very little, my son knew what storytelling was about; he knew there was a problem that needed to be solved and he would wait in anticipation of the ending.

WHY DO CHILDREN LOVE READING and storytelling? Babies love it simply because they love you performing any activity in close proximity to them. They love to hear your familiar voice and to look at something very close to them – whether it's your face, your hands or the colourful pages of a book. It doesn't matter that they don't understand the words in the beginning. Very quickly they will start to associate the words 'book' or 'story' with a happy and reassuring activity.

As they get older, young children start to get ideas from stories and books, and develop them in their play. They start by imitating things they have seen and heard that are of interest to them – so they might try to draw or make a farm or jungle they have seen in a book, or simply imitate things they have heard you say when you've been reading to them or telling them a story. Through this process they begin to *imagine* – they might imagine in the simplest way what life is like on a farm, for instance, or living with dinosaurs; they might imagine a penguin in Antarctica, or a rabbit lost in a vegetable patch, or a mouse scurrying through a deep dark wood. When they hit on something that really sparks their interest and imagination you will find they want to keep developing the same topic or idea. They'll ask questions about it and talk about it constantly. Encourage this by reading or telling the same story again and again if requested and talking about it with them.

This need not be a chore. Reading and storytelling can be one of the most relaxing and enjoyable activities to engage in with a child. For a start, you get to sit down in a comfortable spot, like a bed or a rocking chair or on cushions on the floor. If you are reading a book to them, all you have to do is open it and the entertainment begins. You just guide them through it – reading the words on the page if you wish or making up your own variations. If you are telling your own stories you don't even have to open a book; just open your mouth and start talking to them. You could think of an interesting incident that happened to you or your child and tell them about it. Or retell a story you've heard someone else tell, like my mother did with the fairytale about the Little Red Hen. (See page 32 for more on storytelling techniques.)

I can't emphasise enough the importance of engaging in these activities with your child. The more they feel your closeness, hear your voice and watch your face as you speak the words, see pictures at close range, touch and turn the pages of a book, the better. (The importance of sensory experiences, like reading, is discussed further in Chapter 7.) Through all this wonderful sensory stimuli they learn language, develop their speech, acquire knowledge, recognise shapes, practise fine-motor skills, and learn to listen, concentrate and observe. That's quite a lot of skills to gain from such a relaxing and happy activity! And these are the skills they will ultimately need when they start to read themselves. This might all be a little hard to comprehend if you are immersed in your child's very early years, when learning to read seems such a long way off. But recent research is in no doubt. According to a recent UK House of Commons report on *Teaching Children to Read* (see Further Reading):

The stimuli a child experiences before the time he or she enters primary school and begins to be taught to read formally are vital to success in reading.

When my then five-year-old was about to start school, I have to confess I was slightly anxious. We had been reading to him regularly for years, and engaging him in all sorts of activity and discussion, yet he still didn't seem interested in the words on the page. Had we really helped him learn to read?

The question I should have been asking myself was not whether we'd helped him learn to read, but whether we'd helped to *prepare him for reading when he started school.* Children aren't suddenly taught how to read. The ongoing debates and discussion about learning to read at least make one thing clear: reading is a very complex skill. It relies on the presence of so many other skills that children develop gradually during their early years through activities like reading and storytelling.

Stories and books aren't the only activities that will develop your child's reading skills. In fact, we hope that most of the games and ideas in this book will help in some way to prepare your child for reading at the appropriate time for him. But reading and storytelling may have the most profound effect on your child's *attitude* to reading in the longer term. Children must *want* to read. As discussed, very young children are naturally drawn to activities like reading and storytelling because they like looking at a distraction immediately in front of them, hearing us talk and being close to us. Try to build on these innate desires. Children will continue to love reading if, through the books and stories you choose and the way you talk to them when engaging in such activities, you capture their attention, develop their interest in a plethora of topics and spark their imagination.

BOOKS, BOOKS AND MORE BOOKS

You can introduce books from a very early age. When my son was four months old he moved his arms and legs excitedly whenever a book was placed in front of him, and an earnest look appeared on his face as he began to focus on the pages. He soon became familiar with two or three books. We started by pointing out just one or two things on each page. I still recall the thrill we experienced when, after showing him a book called *The Farm* for a number of months, repeating the names of some of the animals and asking him from time to time, 'Where's the *horse*, where's the *horse*?', he slowly moved his tiny hand towards the horse on the page. It was the beginning of an endless fascination with books.

So, how do you foster an interest in books?

THE STORYTIME ROUTINE

Try to make books a part of your child's day, preferably by reading to him at a set time, such as before bed – as well as at other times, when the opportunity arises. This way, books become routine for him. As we discussed in the previous chapter, young children love the familiarity of a routine. Most importantly, the reading routine needs to be stimulating (see 'How to read', page 30) – not in a loud and heavy-handed way, but in a way that encourages a positive attitude to reading so it becomes a natural thing for him to want to do on his own.

WHICH BOOKS?

Be discriminating – don't just read something for the sake of it. If you don't like the book, you will have a hard time sparking your child's interest in it. There are many excellent age-appropriate children's booklists available – seek advice from your local library or bookstore. I'd thoroughly recommend taking your child to a library on a regular basis. It is normally a happy excursion, and will also help you to work out what kinds of books appeal most to your child before you buy. Many libraries and bookstores have regular 'storytime' sessions for children as well.

Baby books

The best books for babies are made of cloth or have thick cardboard pages. He will soon want to grab at the book and is likely to tear pages of ordinary books. See if you can find books with high colour contrasts or shiny/sparkly paper on some of the images to attract his attention. Look for books with different textures to touch, buttons to press and flaps to lift, or 'song' books like *The Wheels on the Bus* that you can sing to him while he is looking at the pictures. 'Point and say' books, with simple photographs of people, animals and other familiar things, are also very appealing.

Familiar themes and characters

As your child gets older and more interested in the characters in a story, start choosing books about animals and children and what they do in a world with which the child is familiar – for example, going to pre-school, the doctor, the zoo or the beach, or getting ready for sleep. These stories particularly appeal to children aged two to four years. An element of naughtiness or bad behaviour in the story always seems to strike a chord with this age group, too – Belinda the cow who refused to be milked; Franklin the turtle's bad day; the little bear who wouldn't go to sleep; Madeline who *knew so well how to frighten Miss Clavel.*

Non-fiction

Young children also love non-fiction books on any number of topics. Every child is different, so try to get a feel for what topics attract your child before you buy. If he enjoys playing with a train set or travelling on a train, try to find a book about trains. If he likes looking at plants and touching leaves, grass and flowers, focus on that topic. Most young children love to look at animals, so find books about animals that interest him and teach him their names, where they live and what they eat. These books can be introduced at any age. Some of these books contain a lot of factual information that will be too much for a young child, but don't be put off; the pictures are often excellent and will give you a lot to talk about. And, as your child gets older and more interested in hearing more of the facts, these books will continue to be useful. You'll be surprised at the books that turn out to be your child's favourites at various stages!

Nursery rhymes, rhyming stories and poems

Include these in your repertoire of reading materials, especially rhymes that are funny and have lots of predictable and repetitive patterns. Your child will gradually start to memorise these without you even noticing. Start off with illustrated books of traditional nursery rhymes (like Humpty Dumpty and Hickory Dickory Dock) and gradually move on to other rollicking reads such as Dr Seuss (*The Cat in the Hat* and others) and the wonderful books by Julia Donaldson (*The Gruffalo, Room on the Broom* and others). The rhyme and repetition help your child to predict what comes next. After a few readings, he'll love to finish the rhyming sentences if you leave off the last word:

Humpty Dumpty sat on a wall
Humpty Dumpty had a great . . .

By age four you can start to point to the rhyming word ('fall') on the page as they say it. This will help make reading a natural and spontaneous activity for them.

HOW TO READ

Much has been written about the skill of reading aloud to children. Not many of us are required to read aloud at work so slipping into the role of narrator at home may not be easy. Reading aloud in a manner that is interesting for children without over-stimulating them (especially just before bed!) takes some thought and practice.

Young children are particularly responsive to different speech sounds so think about varying your voice and experimenting with a wide range of sounds – high and low, soft and loud, long drawn out sounds (like *miaowwwww*) and short sounds (like *woof*). Experiment with fiction books by speaking in a different voice for the different characters in the story.

When reading Arnold Lobel's *Frog and Toad are Friends* series to our son I tried to use a slow, croaky voice for Toad and a more sprightly voice for Frog. On occasion I would forget which voice I was supposed to be using and switch them around, but my son was quick to correct me. I found his attention to this quite extraordinary; it really mattered to him that I spoke with the correct voice for each character.

You don't need to read the story straight through from beginning to end. As you read, take some time to do the following:

Discuss the pictures

Talk to your child about what you can see on the page. Once his speech starts to develop, ask him questions about what is going on in the picture:

What colour is the car?

Can you see the little dog under the table?

How many balloons is the girl holding?

What is the monkey eating?

Discuss the subject

As your child gets older, discuss the book's subject matter. This will encourage him to ask questions. Non-fiction books can be particularly good for these discussions. Again, try to tap into subjects that particularly interest your child. Catering to our son's interest in dinosaurs, we ended up with more than a few books about these creatures. Aged three, he frequently asked us how the dinosaurs died out. I guess it is a sensible question to ask if you are small and wanting some assurance that these frightening beasts aren't going to appear on your doorstep one day. In his braver moments, however, he seemed genuinely sorry that they had disappeared.

Look at the words

A book's pictures will remain of primary interest to children throughout their early years. It is important to encourage this by choosing books with good illustrations. But about age four, however, you can also start pointing to the words on the page. You don't need to use your finger under every word as you read; just point out one or two words every so often. Then your child will start to focus naturally on print rather than feeling forced to do so when he starts school.

STORYTELLING – YOU HAVE AN AUDIENCE!

With the explosion of print and electronic media over the last century, we have become overwhelmed by the stories and entertainment provided by others. Many of us have forgotten about our ability to entertain children with our own storytelling skills. In our obsession with the present, we don't reminisce so much any more, especially in front of the kids. And yet, when we give it some thought, we all have a wealth of experiences and tales that can be turned into little stories to share with them. As well as passing on a bit of our past to them, this is also a very appealing form of entertainment, even for very young children. You will be amazed at how interested a three-year-old will be in a story that involves him or people with whom he is familiar. It needn't necessarily be funny or about anything that you or I would consider particularly remarkable. The simple fact that the story is about people he knows or things that happened in a world that he recognises is usually enough to engage him.

As my son became more familiar with the concept of storytelling through my mother's versions of the Little Red Hen (page 23), she started to tell him more stories about funny or strange things that had happened to him or his parents or other family members or friends. He soon knew that if he asked the right questions – and begged just a little bit – he would get a good yarn from her.

Of course, there is an art to storytelling. Like any good public speaker, you need to work at capturing your audience's attention – even more so when your audience is less than a metre tall. The aim at the beginning is simply to familiarise them with the routine of storytelling (in the same way as they become familiar with the routine of reading books). When making up your own little story, keep the following in mind:

Choose the subject

Keep the subject matter very simple to start with. Perhaps you could recount a little incident that once happened to your child. Think of something he found funny or surprising, something he was once afraid of or did not want to do, something bad or unusual that happened one day, or a little mystery that needed to be solved.

Use repetition

Many classic children's storybooks involve a repetitive element – either they repeat the same phrase during the course of the story (for example, 'I'll huff and I'll puff and I'll blow your house down' in *The Three Little Pigs*, or 'Someone's been eating *my* porridge' in *Goldilocks and the Three Bears*) or they involve a recurring theme. One of the simplest examples of a recurring theme is a story about a lost toy or animal. (The recurring theme is where to look next for the lost property.) Many children's storybooks are based on this theme, from very simple stories like *Where's Spot?* (Is he behind the door? Is he under the bed? Is he in the cupboard?), to more complex stories about getting lost while playing hide-and-seek or looking for a family pet that's gone missing. You can easily make up a tale about something similar that happened in your family.

Also, children are likely to want to hear their favourite stories repeated again and again. As much as you'd like to move onto other tales, indulge them and use the opportunity to reinforce phrases and concepts, and to discuss the story further.

Use your child's name

When you are telling the story, use your child's name – and that of family members or friends – as much as possible ('Eliza did this . . . then she did that . . .'). Describe their character or how they were feeling ('Oliver liked dinosaurs . . . He was very excited.')

Add interest

Use some actions – such as moving two fingers to show someone walking – and facial expressions to add drama and show feelings or moods. And make the story *sound* interesting by varying your tone of voice. For example, say, 'Ben didn't like that sound', in a deep, concerned voice or, 'Guess what we found in the drawer!' in a high, astonished voice.

Below are four examples of the kind of simple stories you might recount to your child. Hopefully they will remind you of similar events in your family's life. The stories have been written to appeal to a child who is about three years old. If your child is older or younger you can increase or decrease the length and complexity as appropriate.

Once upon a time there was a little boy called Henry . . .

and Henry was walking to the Museum in London with his Uncle Simon. *[Use your fingers to show that he was walking.]* Henry wanted to go and see the dinosaur exhibition. Henry talked about the exhibition all the time because he just loved dinosaurs.

The museum was a long way from his house but Henry was so excited about seeing the exhibition that he didn't care how far he had to walk. He went inside the museum and Uncle Simon asked the man at the door where the dinosaurs were. The man said:

'Follow the dinosaur signs to the room at the end of this corridor. There is a model of a big dinosaur called a tyrannosaurus rex right at the entrance to the exhibition.'

They followed the dinosaur signs to a room with a model of

tyrannosaurus rex outside. They were about to go in when suddenly Henry heard a big, loud, booming noise. He turned around and saw a video that was showing visitors what was on inside the exhibition. The video showed a huge dinosaur moving his head slowly from side to side and making a very loud roaring noise.

Henry did *not* like that sound. Even though he loved dinosaurs, Henry was frightened by that sound. He turned around and started to run away as fast as his little legs would carry him. The kind man at the door tried to explain to Henry that the dinosaur was not real. Uncle Simon tried to explain to Henry that the dinosaur was not real. But no one could help him change his mind. So Henry never saw the dinosaur exhibition in London.

Instead, Henry asked Uncle Simon to take him to another room to see the bugs and the reptiles, and he was very happy.

Once upon a time, your mother used to live in New Zealand . . .

She was only three years old. One day her parents told her that she and her older brother Jack were going to have a big surprise. They were going to get in a little aeroplane and fly over the volcano. Everyone knew about this volcano in New Zealand. There were pictures of it in the newspaper, there were pictures of it on the television. There was red fire and black smoke coming out of the top of this volcano. Sophie and Jack could see the volcano from their house and they could sometimes see the black smoke coming out of it.

Sophie and Jack were very excited. When they woke up in the morning, they got dressed quickly and had their breakfast. Sophie kept jumping up and down and saying all the time:

'Going to see the volcano, going to see the volcano!'

Everyone finished their breakfast, put on their jackets and drove out in the car to the edge of the lake where there was a little plane waiting for them. Sophie was still saying:

'Going to see the volcano, going to see the volcano!'

They got out of the car and there was the pilot waiting for them with the little plane. They got into the plane with the pilot. They settled into their seats and put on their seat belts. Then the plane made a loud noise as it started up and took off into the sky. But Sophie soon felt her eyes closing and before she knew what was happening, she was sound asleep. Jack was looking out the window and saw the volcano as they climbed higher and higher. He kept trying to wake Sophie as they got close but she was sound asleep. He could not wake her up so he had to leave her asleep. Jack was amazed to see the red fire and the black smoke on the top of the volcano.

Then the plane had to come back down. When it landed, it made a very loud noise as the pilot put the brakes on. Sophie woke up suddenly, sat up and said:

'Where's the volcano? Where's the volcano?'

Her brother told her she had missed it because she was sound asleep and now the plane was down on the ground again. She was very, very disappointed.

But because she had had such a good sleep, Sophie suddenly felt very hungry, so she was very happy when her mum said:

'Let's go and have a picnic lunch on the grass!'

The year of the dog

While you were in Hong Kong watching the celebrations and parade for Chinese New Year and the Year of the Dog, I went for a little walk down my street. It was late at night and quite dark. I went to the end of the street then turned round to walk back again. As I got halfway back up the street I saw something quite big standing under a street light. It looked like a little horse but NO, of course it wasn't a horse in my street – it was a very big dog. Well, it looked big to me. I had never seen this dog before.

I was a little bit frightened so I thought I would walk on the footpath on the opposite side of the street, in the shadows of the trees, so that the dog wouldn't see me. The dog didn't move but it kept looking at me. When I got past it, I kept looking back to see if it had gone – but it didn't move. It just kept staring at me.

I got home and was sitting inside on the bottom stair taking off my shoes when something appeared at the front door. It was the big dog. He didn't make a sound. He just looked at me with his head on one side in such a sweet way. I think he was trying to say:

'I am lonely. I am lost. I like you. Will you let me come into your house?'

Well, I didn't think I should let him come into my house. So I went out and had a look at his name tag. I rang his owners but there was no one at home so I left a message on their machine. The big dog kept standing there. I said goodnight to him and shut the door very gently. Next morning, who do you think was asleep on our front door mat? Yes, the big dog. And he looked very pleased to see me again.

Now isn't that a funny way to start the Year of the Dog?

Once upon a time our family had a little kitten . . .

called Zadi. She was very pretty. Her fur was chocolate brown and soft and silky. She looked like a princess. She walked like a princess. Everyone loved Zadi except Patrick, who thought she looked like a rat.

One night, we had visitors for dinner, and everyone wanted to meet our new little kitten. But no one could find her. She had disappeared. We walked through every room, downstairs then upstairs. No Zadi. We looked in the cupboard. No Zadi. We looked under the bed. No Zadi. We looked behind the door. No Zadi.

Suddenly, someone heard a very faint *miaow*. Everyone crept around on tiptoe, trying not to make a sound. Everyone was listening very carefully so they could work out where the *miaow* was coming from.

Kim thought it was coming from the study, so she walked into the study and stood in the middle of the room. She went over to the desk. She listened again. Yes, a tiny *miaow*. Very gently, she opened the drawer of the desk. She heard another *miaow* and there at the back of the drawer was our dear little kitten. Kim talked very softly to Zadi and told her not to worry.

'It's all right, Zadi. We'll look after you.'

Then Kim lifted Zadi carefully out of the drawer. She could feel the kitten's heart beating very fast because Zadi was very little and very frightened. Kim cuddled her till she felt better and then let her rest on the lounge for the rest of the night.

Over the next few months, Zadi grew up very quickly. She loved to jump up on the top of a very tall cupboard in the dining room whenever there were visitors in the house. We called that her party trick. She was not happy when the family went on holidays. She seemed to know we were going away whenever she saw the suitcases being packed into the car. Once, when she saw the suitcases being packed, she crept back inside the house when no one was looking . . . **and what do you think happened next?**

As your child becomes more familiar with storytelling, see if he is interested in finishing the story himself or guessing how it might end.

3. A is for . . .

LETTERS AND WORDS

*One of my very earliest memories is the wonder
I experienced when I acquired my first set of wooden bricks,
each with a letter on it, and whenever I visit one of my small
friends with such a set, I squat on the floor, the better to shuffle
the pieces about; I would not exchange for all the gold of the
Indies the look on the face of a child who has just made the
connection between c a t and his furry friend.*

Bernard Levin, IF YOU WANT MY OPINION

THERE ARE SO MANY THINGS you may have thought about
buying to try to get your child focused on letters and words – alphabet books, puzzles, charts, blocks, posters, floor mats and tracing sets,
toys that repeat 'a is for apple' (and many other agonising sounds) ad
nauseam, flashcards, word games and fridge magnets. Indeed, some
of us *have* bought vast quantities of these things, only to discover that
many end up largely ignored, used under protest or used for a different

purpose altogether. We've all tried to hide our despair but occasionally our frustrations surface:

SHE'S JUST BURIED ALL HER MAGNETIC LETTERS
IN THE SANDPIT!

Don't despair. In this sea of letters and cacophony of talking toys, keep in mind the simple purpose of getting your child to focus on letters and words. We read for *meaning*. What's important ultimately is not just that your child can say the word 'cat' when she sees it, but that, as Levin says in the quote above, she *makes the connection* between the word 'cat' and her furry friend. Only then does she start to understand that words represent real things.

Identifying a word on paper and then connecting it with its meaning is a hugely complex skill for a young child. Getting to that stage requires a solid foundation of other skills, including language and speech skills, hearing and listening skills, memory skills, and an ability to distinguish shapes and patterns. It also requires a knowledge and understanding of many, many words. As mentioned in the previous chapter, the process of building up these reading skills happens very naturally and gradually in the early years through all kinds of play and discussion with your child.

With this in mind, we must begin the topic of letters and words with a word of caution. It is easy as a parent to become a little fixated with our child's progress in recognising letters and then words. We also tend to fall into the trap of wanting to see fairly immediate and direct results of our teaching efforts. So it may give us a thrill to see our two-year-old point to and recite the letters of the alphabet. But we don't necessarily derive the same thrill from watching her concentrate on a story for five minutes. In fact, although five minutes of concentration may not be such an obvious achievement, it is critical to the skill of eventually learning to read.

As a parent, and having been bombarded and baffled by different methods for teaching letters and words to young children, what I've learnt is this: by all means play games at home that focus on recognising letters of the alphabet and, later, the written word. (We offer some suggestions in Chapter 10, and you will get ideas from many other sources on this topic as well.) Find out the approach taken at your child's preschool – it's important to talk to the staff about what they are doing and why, and to try to be consistent with this approach at home. But keep some perspective on these activities. They are not the only activities that will prepare your child for reading when she starts school. Nor should they be played particularly with the goal of reading in mind; rather, play them for their own entertainment value. If your child enjoys playing the games, then that's great, but if not, save them for another day. Rest assured that if you're doing the kinds of things we talk about throughout the book, you will already be doing a huge amount to help your child build the skills ultimately needed for reading.

LISTENING FOR LETTERS

The most basic letters and words games help your child to listen for the sound of the first letter of a word. For example, by age two-and-a-half, you can take your child by the hand and look for things around the room that begin with 'c' (cup, cot, cat, car), emphasising the sound 'c' at the beginning of each word. This is the idea of the game **Listening for letters** on page 133. The game **What does it start with?** on page 135 builds on this skill.

SOUNDING OUT LETTERS – THE ENGLISH PUZZLE

But what sound should your child be listening for exactly? How do you introduce your child to the letter 'a' when it doesn't always sound like the 'a' in 'apple'? When talking with your child, do you call letters by their names ('a', 'b', 'c'), or by the way they sound? And if you say the letters of the alphabet phonetically (i.e. as they sound), what *is* the sound exactly?

Before you collapse in confusion, let me illustrate this difficulty with a story about my first experience with the topic of phonetics. When our first child was two years old, I attended his Montessori preschool in Hong Kong for a lesson on how to help children say the letters of the alphabet. I had wondered whether I was wasting my time attending this class. After all, unlike most of the Chinese parents in the classroom, I had been speaking, reading and writing English for 30-plus years. But in that lesson, I found myself learning the phonetic sounds of the English alphabet for the first time!

We were taught to whisper letters like 'c', 'h' and 't', and to say 'f' like we were blowing out candles and 'm' like we had just eaten something delicious – 'mmmm'. As I looked around the room at my earnest and eager classmates, I thought once more about the complexities of the English language. Here we were learning the phonetic sounds and yet only 50 per cent of English words are phonetically spelt. Weren't we over-simplifying things a bit here? Not necessarily . . .

The use of phonics helps children identify the most basic sounds of the alphabet. A baby starts to imitate us by using phonetic sounds within a few months. For example, you might hear the sounds 'm', 'b' and 'g'. Helping your child to listen for these basic sounds and then, as she gets older, to gradually connect these sounds with letters, is a logical next step. To say a letter phonetically, sound it out as you would say it in the words given in the chart below. *Many consonants, like 't', are whispered.*

Sound Chart

a	apple	h	hen	o	orange	v	van
b	bed	i	ink	p	pig	w	web
c	cat	j	jug	q	queen	x	fox
d	dog	k	kite	r	red	y	yellow
e	egg	l	leg	s	sun	z	zebra
f	fan	m	mum	t	table		
g	goat	n	net	u	umbrella		

Listening for letters at the start of words is a big step. There is no need to rush this stage. Some children will love playing the game **Listening for letters** (page 133) for months. Others may not be interested to begin with, but might take to it more quickly at a later stage. Be led by your child rather than by any suggested age guides.

LOOKING AT LETTERS

Once she is happily running around the room identifying objects that begin with the letter 'c', you can start to show her what this letter looks like (see **Looking at letters** on page 141). Use a lower-case magnetic or wooden 'c' to start with, or write it down for her on a card.

This is the stage when, in a typical Montessori preschool environment, your child might be introduced to what are often known as 'sandpaper letters' – lower-case letters made of sandpaper and mounted on little boards. The idea behind sandpaper letters is to provide the child with a tactile experience (feeling the shape of the letter) as well as a visual and aural one (looking at the letter and watching and listening to you say its sound). Receiving information about the letter by using various sensory powers *at the same time* helps her to remember it. (The importance of receiving information from all the senses is discussed further in Chapter 7). The **Looking at letters** game assumes you will be using either magnetic or wooden letters at home. But if your handwriting and cutting skills are better than mine, you can easily make up your own letter cards. They don't have to be made of sandpaper – any material that provides some sort of tactile experience for your child while learning letters is good.

LOOKING AT WORDS

As your child gets more familiar with the sound, look and feel of letters, you can start to introduce some activities that focus on words. In my experience the best age to start this is around four years. By this stage, not only are children more familiar with the sound and shape of the alphabet letters, but they also have a good knowledge and understanding of many, many words. They have heard words used in various contexts and become familiar with some written words – for example, they might recognise 'dinosaur' because it has appeared often in their books or their play. Through this very natural process they will have started to recognise some words by sight and to connect them with their meanings.

This is not to say that children can't recognise words before the age of four. They can learn to recognise the shape of words in much the same way as they recognise the shape of other things (shown to them in a picture book, for example) from a very young age – if they have been trained to do so.

I admit to being mildly perplexed when one friend told me her two-year-old recognised words like 'strawberry' on a word card and waved his arms excitedly whenever these cards appeared in front of him. Some people regard these word cards (or 'flashcards', as they have become known) as a legitimate method of teaching toddlers to read; others argue that the ability to recognise a word on a card is point-less unless there is some context that also enables the child to grasp its meaning. And so the debates go on ... If you want my opinion, keep some perspective on *any one* method that claims to teach your child to read.

Recognising the shape or pattern of a word is certainly one skill that will help prepare a child for reading. But, as mentioned earlier, a child must also begin to connect the written word with its meaning. This won't happen much before age four, and only through the develop-ment of a vast array of skills. Even then, not all children will greet word cards with quite the same level of enthusiasm as my friend's child. My own children certainly didn't – unless the cards were incorporated into other activities they liked doing. So, for instance, they enjoyed a game of hide-and-seek with word cards, as in the game **Find the 'c' in 'cat'** on page 158. And they liked to 'walk the talk' by jumping over words on the floor when they recognised them (as in **Jump the word** on page 173). They were also eager to read clues on cards as part of a treasure hunt (see page 159).

The more you write down words in front of your child as part of an activity or discussion, the more you'll help her to understand that words represent things.

When I was working, my then three-year-old used to spend an hour a week after preschool at my friend's house. Each time, she would send him home with four or five little coloured cards containing words and drawings of things they had discussed together. So, one week they might have talked about 'plastic', 'roof', 'London' and 'cactus', and he'd come home with those words – and accompanying pictures – on his cards. The purpose was not to focus his attention on reading the words as such, but to expand his vocabulary, help him understand the meaning of the words, and familiarise him with the concept of writing things down.

Through activities like this one and **No Dogs Allowed!** (see page 161) – always done as part of play and discussion, not as a formal lesson – a child's basic understanding of the complex skills of reading, and also writing, gradually comes together.

4. In the Playhouse
ROLE PLAY AND MAKE-BELIEVE

A grown man entertaining three raccoons, treating them like real ladies. Instinctively colluding in the conspiracy of their fiction, taking care not to decimate it with adult carelessness. Or affection. It is after all so easy to shatter a story. To break a chain of thought. To ruin a fragment of a dream being carried around carefully like a piece of porcelain.

Arundhati Roy, THE GOD OF SMALL THINGS

IN HER NOVEL *The God of Small Things*, Arundhati Roy shows an uncanny understanding of what is important to a child. The 'three raccoons' referred to in the excerpt above are three small children who look like raccoons because they have smudged their mother's forbidden make-up around their eyes in an attempt to pass themselves off as 'Hindu ladies'. The man is Velutha, a factory-worker. All dressed up, the children know that Velutha will indulge them in their fantasy world – he will know what to say and how to act. So, rather than any other adult, they seek him out. And he does not disappoint. When they introduce themselves as 'Mrs Pillai, Mrs Eapen and Mrs Rajagopalan' he treats them with 'the utmost courtesy' and engages them in adult-like conversation. And they love him for it.

It comes completely naturally to young children to imitate adult behaviour. Putting on a pilot's hat, wandering around the house with a pair of oversized sandshoes and a tennis racquet, befriending a favourite soft toy, pushing around a toy stroller or shopping trolley (even if it's just a cardboard box), building a playhouse, having a tea party or talking to an imaginary friend all constitute forms of role play. In these activities you will observe your child start to repeat things that you – and others – have done or said.

A LOVE OF FANCIFUL CHARACTERS

But is children's role play simply about copying our behaviour? I started to consider this after my second child was born. Even in his first year he would take great delight in watching me kiss his toy bear goodnight as I was putting him to bed. I would say goodnight to the bear and he would then give it a big hug. Why did he enjoy this activity so much? Part of his pleasure was clearly the comfort he derived from a bedtime ritual (as discussed in Chapter 1). But his delight suggested there was more to it than that. What appeared to tickle his fancy was the idea that his bear had come to life and was *involved* in part of his daily routine. I found this extraordinary. Here, in the quietness of his room each night, I seemed to be witnessing the 'magic of Disney', no less. I don't mean that I was dangling a bit of Disney merchandise in front of him. Rather, I mean that my son's delight in watching a little toy bear go to bed was the first sign of his natural affinity with fanciful characters.

My son wasn't simply interested in watching a toy bear copy what he was doing; he was interested in this bear as a little friend – someone he could interact with and derive comfort from. Inventing and interacting with such characters through role play is one of the most glorious characteristics of childhood. Walt Disney recognised this and built a business around it. Beatrix Potter realised it in her timeless tales of little animals engaged in human activities. And one of the world's most popular ballets, Tchaikovsky's *Nutcracker*, is about a little girl's toy that comes to life at Christmas time.

You can nurture this love of fantastic, fanciful characters by engaging your child in a variety of role-play activities with a favourite toy. (This is the focus of the games **Party time!**, page 129; **Goodnight**, page 118; and **Feed the animals**, page 131.) You can also involve their toys in other parts of their daily routine. For example, when you get home after an outing with your child, you could say to his well-travelled soft friend:

Now, Big Bear, we take our shoes off inside and we wash our hands before lunch.

This helps to reinforce your household routine in a way that appeals to the child. You can reinforce manners in the same way. For example, when playing together with a toy rabbit you could say things like:

You mustn't do that, Peter Rabbit. That is unkind. Please could you share your toys?

Or:

Peter Rabbit, what do you say when I give something to you? That's right – you say thank you.

You don't need to purchase a lot of toys to encourage this love of role play. Some children don't want any friend other than a familiar piece of blanket or a small raggedy donkey. Some will make up an imaginary friend and just start talking to it – and keep talking to it. Some will suddenly 'see' bears through the cracks in the fence.

When my son was three years old, my mother came to stay. Every morning at breakfast, she would circle her arm around in front of him, opening and shutting her thumb and forefinger – like a bird's beak. This make-believe bird became known as Lily. Lily soon became a favourite friend. Each morning Lily would fly in and ask her young friend if she could have breakfast with him. She would fly around and above him, chattering all the time, before eventually landing on his shoulder. It was very important to my son that Lily had a funny high-pitched voice. From then on, he always recognised that voice as Lily's.

IMAGINATIVE ROLE PLAY

As children get older, read more books, watch more DVDs, interact with more people and have more experiences outside the home, they will start to imitate all sorts of actions and forms of behaviour. Through imitation, children gradually start to imagine what it is like to *be* someone or something else. They may pretend to be a doctor, pilot, farmer or zookeeper; they might hop about like a kangaroo or snap their arms together like a crocodile's jaws. Other roles may take you completely by surprise. My then four-year-old son, for example, would pretend to be the broadcaster David Attenborough, imitating Attenborough's charismatic commentary as he sorted through his vast collection of plastic sea animals.

Try to go along with whatever role plays take your child's fancy, talking back at him in a similar voice or asking questions about who or what he is. Give him things – dress-ups and other objects – that allow him to indulge in another world. (This is the focus of the games **Playhouse**, page 143; **Dress-ups**, page 132; **Schools**, page 162; and **I'm a doctor**, page 163). You will soon veer off into your own way of playing similar games and your child will give you leads for new ideas.) Role play needn't be costly. A couch can serve as a heliport. A rug can be the sea. The legs of a table and chairs can be a forest for crawling through and hiding in.

THE ROLE OF ROLE PLAY

If you nurture your child's love of role play, he will love you for it. That should be reason enough, but if you are looking for other reasons to engage in role play with your child, read on.

Pretending to be someone or something else will help your child express himself with confidence, particularly if he is performing to an 'audience' – even if it is only you. Having fanciful friends also helps children establish a sense of self-worth because it allows them to feel superior for a change. Children are used to being told what to do, but in these make-believe worlds they're in charge, and they love it. They can tell their 'friends', or other people – including you – what to do, and you should try to go along with this to encourage them (within reasonable boundaries, of course!).

Role play also helps with language development. Young children will be prompted to expand their vocabulary by using words they've heard others using, as well as ones that relate to whatever world they're playing in. Doctors will need to talk about hospitals and people who are sick – coughing, having a fever or getting a vaccine. Shop-keepers have to tend to the cash register, money and customers. Bus drivers make stops, and have all kinds of passengers who get on and off and pay their fares. This word-learning will be fun because the child is motivated to both interact with these worlds and talk about them.

By indulging him in these fantasy worlds – and, most importantly, by playing an appropriate role yourself – you can also encourage some basic social and emotional awareness. By putting himself – literally, sometimes! – into the shoes of another (whether that be the shoes of a fireman, doctor, mother or sick friend), your child will start to see things from another's perspective, develop an interest in what other people do and respond to their needs. You can help him start to inter-pret basic human emotions – happiness, sadness, fear, anger, surprise and so on. He can begin to learn how to behave in particular circum-stances (for example, in a hospital, library or restaurant, when meeting someone for the first time or when seeing someone in distress). He can learn about manners. He can learn about sharing. He can learn to wait his turn. He will start to ask questions. In short, he will begin to under-stand the basics of decent human behaviour.

These might sound like rather ambitious goals to achieve while engaging in a simple and seemingly uneventful game of dress-ups or shops. But, as with all learning in these early years, emotional learning is ingrained through small and repetitive interactions, repeated regu-larly over a period of years and adapted to suit the age and stage of a young child. Don't expect too much too quickly. Remember how long it takes to ingrain words like 'please' and 'thank you' into a child's speech at the appropriate time. As parents of young children know, we start this as early as possible with our children – we can't help ourselves. The same can be said for basic emotional lessons for a child. In *Emotional Intelligence*, well-known author and psychologist David Goleman (see Further Reading) writes:

Emotional learning begins in life's earliest moments and continues throughout childhood. All the small exchanges between parent and child have an emotional subtext, and in the repetition of these messages over the years children form the core of their emotional outlook and capabilities.

So when you are engaging in a game of 'doctors' or taking a favourite soft toy to the vet, play the role of the soothing doctor sometimes and say things to the patient like, 'Don't be frightened. I won't hurt you.' Your child will soon be doing the same when he's the doctor or vet and observes the worried face of his patient (if it's you) or the quiver of his toy bear. Or, when having a party for his soft toys (as in **Party time** on page 129) you could show that one animal is sad that he can't come because he is sick. Or, when pretending to feed his favourite plastic farm animals you could show how each must wait its turn to be fed or how one animal might get cross if another animal takes his food. Any such drama will be highly appealing to a young child, and at the same time help his social and emotional development.

While some of us are natural actors, many of us cringe at the thought of playing a role, even if the audience is only our child. We just don't feel comfortable making a special voice for a fireman, for instance, let alone wearing a fireman's hat. Worse, we may completely fail to appreciate our child's interest in make believe worlds and snap him out of these activities too readily with our careless, disinterested or thought-shattering responses:

Mama, rabbit has got a sore tummy. [says our child]

Hurry up, Jack, and get your shoes on. We've got to go. [we respond automatically]

We've all done it. Of course we can't indulge children in these fantasy worlds all of the time. But if this becomes the general way we react to their fanciful friends, stories or other role play ideas, they will soon give up on this most precious form of play. So try not disappoint. If he seeks out your involvement, take a role in these worlds – even if it's only for a minute or two.

Once you have sparked a child's interest and imagination through role play there is no end to its possibilities. Soon he will be dreaming up roles for himself that you haven't thought about since your own childhood – a rocket man, an aquarium keeper or a Mrs Rajagopalan.

5. Counting Them In

NUMBERS AND ORDER

FOR SOME PEOPLE, focusing on numbers is always a pleasure. But many others don't even want to think about maths once they leave school, as it tends to conjure up thoughts of memorising times tables, bothersome long division and hefty algebraic calculations. Maths' reputation certainly suffers a bit in the minds of many of us. But it's not necessarily a lack of ability that explains this. Many of us simply were not encouraged to find the fun beyond the fundamentals we learnt at school and to pursue maths interests.

There has been much talk in recent years about countries that are 'good at maths'. On international comparison tests, for example, students from Asian countries have consistently and substantially outperformed their Western – including Australian – counterparts. Attitudes to the subject may well be influencing these trends. The less we think about numeracy skills and apply them to real-life tasks, the less we encourage our children to do the same.

It's not just up to our schools to solve this problem. Parents, carers and other role models can also prompt many little activities that help a child develop a mathematical mindset. These activities are not about teaching maths on paper; instead, they encourage a child to start to think logically as they go about their daily routines and explore their world. The ideas are surprisingly easy and, as we'll see, can be done with children from a very young age.

YOUNG MATHEMATICAL MINDS

If only we could delve back into our early childhood, we might feel more positive about our own mathematical abilities. Montessori believed that all young children display characteristics of a 'mathematical mind' – although we might not necessarily recognise them as such.

Think about how a baby is attracted to cards and mobiles with simple geometric shapes and patterns. (See Appendix 1, page 177: **While he's watching you** . . .) Observe a toddler's interest in orderly toys – a set of plastic cylinders that fit neatly one inside the other, a set of little blocks that she can stack, or a geometric shape that fits through a similar-shaped hole in a shape-sorter. Witness a child's satisfaction in working out that each piece of a puzzle has a place of its own. It's the precision of these activities that attracts her and her natural sense of order that propels her to find the 'right answer'.

No one would deny the importance of developing these skills. They are important not just for numeracy in the longer term, but for so many other activities that rely on a clear and orderly mind. What many of us don't realise, however, is how easy it is to encourage a young child's 'mathematical tendencies' just by building on what comes naturally. There is no need for a formal set-up or even to write anything down. The development of these natural tendencies can simply become part of your daily interactions with your child.

Talk about numbers

One of the most obvious ways of appealing to a young child's sense of order is to introduce her to numbers and counting. You will be surprised at how much a one-year-old enjoys the familiar sound of counting from one to three, for example, or how much she likes to be handed things *one at a time*. She will soon feel secure in the knowledge that 'three' always comes after 'two' – long before she understands what 'three' means.

We have a friend who very naturally brings numbers into conversation with his grandchildren. The children don't realise what he is up to because he doesn't make a thing of it. As far as they are concerned, he is a great entertainer who loves a bit of fun. But if numbers fit into his latest little tale, he delights in contributing a little to the children's mathematical development. So he might say something like:

Last night, I was busy trying to light the barbecue in the backyard. I'd left some sausages out on the table behind me. Suddenly, I heard a noise and TWO big fat kookaburras swooped down and started pecking at my sausages. Then ONE more kookaburra appeared – two and one make three – so I had THREE naughty kookaburras pecking at my sausages!

Here are some other ways you could incorporate numbers and counting into your daily conversations with your young child:

* Count out loud as you hand coloured fish to her in the bath.
  For example, say:
  Three fish – one [hand her a fish], *two* [hand her a fish], *three*
  [hand her a fish].
  We have three fish.
  In the same way, count out little pieces of fruit as you give them to
  her or put them on her plate.
* Count the dogs you see when you're out walking. For example,
  say:
  *What's that? Look – there is one dog in front of us and another dog
  across the road. We can see two dogs. One, two* [repeat the numbers
  as you point to the dogs].
* Count out loud as you are setting the table:
  How many people do we have for dinner tonight? Let's count [say the
  names of the people and count them].
  *We have three people for dinner tonight. So how many spoons do we
  need?* [Get out the spoons and hand them to your child, one at a
  time, as you say the numbers out loud with her.]
  Also see the game **Three spoons in the box** on page 113.
* Count as you go up the stairs – only one to three to start with.
* As you're putting on her T-shirt, say:
  One arm in, then the other arm – two arms!
  One, two [as you touch her arms].
* Point to a number on a house, letterbox or road sign when you are
  out walking:
  See this number? This is a two. This is the number two.
  Draw a number two in the sand or on the ground using chalk:
  This is a two.
* As you start to play easy board games (like snakes and ladders),
  focus on the pattern of the dots on the die when you shake it.

Count the dots:

You got a two – one, two [as she moves along the board].

❋ Some rhymes and songs make reference to numbers – use these to familiarise your child with numbers. Some have a natural connection with certain activities ('One potato, two potato, three potato, four . . .' while in the kitchen together, or 'Five little ducks' when she's in the bath) but you don't have to be rigid about when you use them. The rhythm and rhyme of the song will help ingrain the sound of the numbers in her memory. (See Appendix 3 for some song ideas.)

Look for order

Of course, numbers and counting are not the only way to appeal to and encourage your child's natural sense of order and clarity. You can comment on things in your child's world that must happen *in order*. For example:

❋ *We put on our shirt before we put on our jacket.*

❋ *We put on our socks before we put on our shoes.*

❋ *We must break the egg before we can whisk it.*

❋ *We must bake the cake before we can ice it.*

And there are plenty of other games and activities, using items you'll have to hand, that help develop the skill of carrying out logical steps in order. For example:

❋ *We need the big block before we can put on the little block.*

❋ *We need this piece of the train track before we can add that piece.*

❋ *We need this piece of the puzzle before that piece will fit.*

As you go about daily activities, do some matching and sorting together. For example:

* Clothes – involve your child in sorting the washing as you match piles of jeans, socks and T-shirts.
* Toys – talk about what you're doing as you sort toys into piles of soft toys, cars and books.
* Small objects – collect things when you are out and about, like shells or seedpods, and let your child sort them into groups.
* Cutlery – let your child help as you put the spoons away here and the forks there.
* Puzzles – work on simple four- and six-piece puzzles that connect together, and as your child's skill develops, increase the number of pieces.

Look for shapes and patterns

You can point out good examples of shapes and patterns when you see them. Your child will continue to notice them even when you have forgotten they are there.

When my son was 18 months, he was fascinated by some steel manhole covers set in the path near our home. In shape, they were perfect circles and squares. I would walk straight over them without thinking, but he would carefully step to one side of each one and excitedly point to 'circle circle' or 'square square'.

Start with the easiest shapes and patterns. For example:

* show her that the clock or her plate is a circle

* cut her toast into a square or a triangle
* find stickers in the shape of hearts, stars and diamonds
* draw simple patterns in dots (like the patterns on dice) or stripes
* arrange blocks in a pattern of blue and red
* point out patterns formed by petals on a flower
* point out the patterns in a puzzle
* point out the different shapes of the moon.

Puzzle it out

Puzzles develop so many useful skills that it's certainly worth having a few in the home and continuing to update them as your child gets older. As mentioned earlier, very young children delight in working out that each piece of the puzzle has a neat little place of its own. Knobbed puzzles for the youngest children not only help them to identify simple shapes but also to refine the finger movements required for drawing and, eventually, writing. As your child gets older you can start to work on simple puzzles that connect together. These help a child recognise patterns and, as the puzzles get more complicated, carry out logical steps *in order* to find the solution. This is quite a collection of skills to gain from such a simple toy. But, much like books, not all puzzles will appeal to your child. Try to discover which puzzle themes attract your child the most.

AS YOUR CHILD GETS OLDER . . .

Look for numbers around you

You can bring numbers and counting into all sorts of practical activities once your child is four or five. Help her to see how numbers fit into the world by asking her to:

* look at the calendar and mark the days of special events, and discuss how far away these events are in time

* look at the numbers on the clock and talk about the time ('o'clock' and 'half-past')
* learn her phone number
* press the numbers on the phone to call grandparents
* answer questions such as:
  × *How many days until your birthday?* (or *until grandma arrives, or until we go to the farm*)
  × *When your sister is four, how old will you be?*
* count all the red cars while travelling in the car
* play with numbers on a large calculator, for example:
  × make patterns such as 1+1+1+1+1+1+1+1+
  × type in her birthday or phone number
* pick out five apples at the supermarket
* break her orange up into segments and talk about how many make up the whole orange
* keep the tally for games by marking down lines on a notepad.

More on quantity, size and shape

You can also start to involve your child in many practical tasks that help her to learn more about quantity, size and shape. For example, you could ask her to:

* sort out plastic animals, Lego pieces or cards into groups of three or four
* if your child has a particular interest in something like blocks, for example, sort out her collection into groups of similar-shaped items
* encourage her to work out the size required to hold certain things:
  × *What shall we use to make a garage for your little red car? Will it fit inside this box?*

* *How many pencils will fit inside this box?*
* *How many seedpods will fit inside this matchbox?*
* *Will we have enough water in this jug to fill these four cups?*
* *Is there enough milk in this jug to put on your cereal?*
* *Which bowl will fit all these potatoes inside it?*

❋ measure quantities of ingredients when she is cooking with you

❋ set the table with you, letting her work out how many knives, forks and spoons are required

❋ compare the size/weight of different grocery items as you put them into the trolley

❋ measure her height and mark it in a permanent place so she can see how much she has grown the next time she is measured (what could be more exciting?).

More on order

Continue to encourage sequential thinking by involving her in tasks that require a number of steps to be carried out in order. For example:

❋ If she shows an interest in gardening, encourage her to draw a plan for a vegetable patch or a flower pot on a piece of paper, then talk about how she needs to prepare the soil before planting the seeds and how they will then need water to grow.

❋ Involve her in three or four steps of a recipe, preferably one with clearly numbered, simple written instructions. Point to the numbers for each step so she can follow along with you. (It doesn't matter that she can't read the words. The idea is just to get her used to following steps in order.)

❋ As she goes about constructing things with Lego or other materials, talk about, for example, how she needs to build the floor and the walls of a house before she adds the roof and the chimney.

Try to involve your child in some of your own 'constructions' as well.

I remember one five-year-old very excitedly telling me about how he helped his grandfather construct a sandpit. It was the construction of it that appealed to him more than the sandpit itself, it seemed. He was still talking about his grandfather's handiwork well after the event.

Even if your interest in DIY disappeared with childhood, you might know other people who are involved in constructing things. It can be very inspiring for a child to observe these activities and, if possible, get involved in some small way.

Make it part of a game

There are many games you can play with four- and five-year-olds that will reinforce the concepts in this chapter. You can set up a pretend shop, for example – make signs to show the cost of each item and use coins to pay for them (see **Shops**, page 168). You can play various board games that involve rolling dice, counting, and moving a counter the correct number of places. You can appeal to your child's sense of order and love of physical activity with the well-used game, **What's the time, Mr Wolf?** (see page 167). She will love to 'feel' the steps she takes as she counts out loud.

If you have encouraged your child's interest in shapes and patterns, this will transfer easily to well-known games such as **Dominoes** (page 164), **Snap!** (page 166) and **Memory** (page 171). In Chapter 10, the rules of these games have been adjusted to suit younger players – but of course you can use whatever rules are familiar to the players in your household. And as with all activities for young children, keep the session short; you will know when your child has had enough.

6. Making It
HANDS AT WORK

IF YOU HAVE BEEN GLIDING through this book thinking that child's play need not be a messy business, then your illusion is about to be shattered. This is the messy chapter. Little hands will plunge into playdough, paint and packet cake-mix. They will construct aquariums, sand castles and some sort of inedible entree (which, of course, you will have to eat). Fingernails will get dirty, sleeves will get wet, milk may get spilt, a change of clothes may be necessary.

If you are like me, just the thought of at least some of these activities will make you grimace a little. I am not an easygoing happy-to-let-the-child-paint-the-walls-blue kind of parent. I am programmed to think about the clean-up effort involved after a craft activity, to worry a little about furniture getting damaged and to care a bit if a favourite bowl is broken. But these are not reasons to skip to the next chapter. Nor are they reasons to over-plasticise your house or heavily restrict your child's access to anything other than 'toys'. Quite the opposite, in fact.

HANDS-ON

A young child does not learn through plastic alone. One of the key (although often forgotten) milestones in his first year is the development of what are rather obscurely termed his 'fine-motor skills'. Put simply, he begins to control things with his hands. Through constant exposure to materials of all different shapes, sizes and textures, a baby starts to learn some very 'fine' skills. He can learn, for example, to:

❋ flick the pages of a magazine through his fingers
❋ open the pages of a cardboard book
❋ rip apart tissues
❋ pick up slithers of grape
❋ squash a small piece of toast
❋ make finger patterns in sand or dirt (or dessert!)
❋ turn something over and check what is on the other side
❋ put objects into a basket and take them out again
❋ twirl the stalk of a flower
❋ spin the wheel on a small car
❋ pick up pieces from a knobbed puzzle
❋ grab a ball and throw it away

The smaller, lighter and more malleable the material, the easier it is for a baby to gain some control over what he is touching. This tactile way of learning about the world is indeed a messy one. It can also be a hair-raising one for adults: little objects, once cleverly grasped, are quickly placed in the mouth (while food, on the other hand, seems to end up everywhere but). Anything that is sticky, squishy, small or easily scattered is a highly appealing target for little hands. So these activities do need to be controlled to protect both child and property – and your own sanity, occasionally. But take the time to observe what really grabs your baby's attention and work out ways in which he can safely explore new things.

Honing the hand skills

You will soon discover that your child – with the right materials at his disposal – is not naturally attracted to chaos at all. Put a one-year-old in a playroom with toys scattered about and he will quickly become bored. He is far happier to discover a neat pile of magazines on a shelf, a stack of little barrels placed one inside the other, or the door of a small cabinet that opens and shuts neatly. His instinct is not to wreak havoc but to try to coordinate his hands to stack, open, close and put things back – imitating what he has seen us do. He practises these new coordinations through a wonderfully instinctive process of repeating little actions with his hands – over and over again.

This urge to repeat seemingly mundane actions often baffles the adult observer. Many of us mistake our child's apparent 'boredom' with his existing toys as a sign that he needs a new toy – something a little flashier, noisier or more 'educational', perhaps – and rush out to find such a thing. Suddenly our house is overrun with toys – and our child is not yet two.

A better approach, in my opinion, is to proceed with caution when browsing through toys advertised for the '1+' and '2+' age range that claim to assist your child's hand–eye coordination and the like. Think carefully about what the toy is designed to achieve and whether an everyday object could safely serve the same purpose. Make the most of the fact that this is possibly the one time in your child's life when he won't be crying out for more toys! A one- or two-year-old will happily hone his hand skills by working with all kinds of ordinary objects:

* emptying cards from an old wallet
* taking pegs or clothes out of a basket and putting them back again
* stacking a pile of blocks
* moving a zipper up and down
* posting pretty much anything through a hole in a box
* pressing the buttons on an old phone or calculator
* opening little plastic bottles and other containers, and trying to close them again
* pouring water from a jug in the bath
* turning a torch on and off
* browsing through a stack of books
* putting pencil to paper, magnet to fridge or sticker to skin . . .

Early creative endeavours

The results of all these dedicated little activities with the hands start to come to the fore by age three. With plenty of encouragement of hand skills in his early years, your three-year-old will make a thrilling discovery: he will become aware of his ability to create something with his hands – *and then to re-create that same thing*. He will learn, for example, to:

* draw something that appeals to him, like a flower, a boat or a fish
* construct some sort of house out of blocks, cardboard boxes or other materials
* shape dough into something vaguely resembling his favourite animal

It is easy to underestimate the significance of this handiwork. An immense amount of mental activity is required to get to this stage. Not only has your child learnt how to control different things with his hands and imitate something shown to him, but he is also beginning to exercise his power to imagine things (i.e. to conjure up images in his mind's eye) and then to reproduce those things with his hands. It is an extraordinary achievement and one that requires constant practice. But practise he will – not instinctively any more but because, like any good artist, he is now motivated to perfect his creative powers.

This self-motivation is remarkable to watch. It is also, however, embarrassingly easy to miss some of your child's early creative endeavours. Young children do not always pause for praise. So, once they have built a very high tower for the first time they may knock it down before you see it, and start again. Similarly, they may draw a perfect image of their favourite animal but then continue to draw over it until the original creation disappears from view.

I almost missed our then three-year-old's first discernable drawing of a whale. (In fact, he'd probably been practising the shape for months but we just hadn't recognised it.) Fortunately my mother caught him drawing it and saved it before it got covered by a sea of blue texta – a sea that, of course, would have made perfect sense to him. After this episode I started to pay much more attention to what my son was drawing. I loved picking up a series of his drawings that were strewn about the place in a moment of creative madness and trying to decipher what they all meant, what he might have been thinking. Often he had drawn the same thing over and over again. He'd rarely be interested in telling me much about the drawings, but as he got older I could occasionally elicit some illuminating responses, such as 'Stars shooting, plants growing' and 'Puffins with blossoms'.

The joy of creation

With lots of encouragement in his early years, an active and happy four-year-old will have more confidence in his creative abilities. By this age he is able to do much more on his own. His creations will be inspired by small and simple pleasures or activities – whether it's collecting things in the garden, looking out the window of a train, watching/helping you cook, looking through books or even pressing the pause button on a video to examine an appealing image in more detail. When his ideas start to flow, be prepared for a frenzy of activity. On a typical day he might want to make a 'scratchy hedgehog', a 'clay dinosaur' and a 'magic house', and cook a 'gingerbread clown'. He will be brimming with ideas on how to fulfil his morning goals – and you will be just starting breakfast.

Of course these tasks are messy; just thinking about them makes us tired sometimes. But as with any creative endeavour and any artist, old or young, whenever ideas start to flow – whether in the sandpit, the office, the shed, the studio or the kitchen – there is always a frenzy of activity. It's a *lack* of mess, and a lack of activity and ideas, that should really concern us. So you have no excuse – go for it! Seize the moments in life to be messy.

WHERE TO START WITH ARTS AND CRAFT

I have never considered myself a 'crafty' person. I can't use scissors easily, activities like papier-mâché and origami have so far eluded me, and the very thought of trying to draw any four-legged animal makes me feel tense. Notwithstanding this baggage, I have tried to acquire some craft skills. With my four-year-old's gentle encouragement, I even felt inspired at times to attempt the outline of an apatosaurus. Against this background, I will share with you a little of what I have learnt about craft and kids.

Like many parents, I made the mistake of assuming that the word 'craft', when applied to childhood activities, must involve things like painting and pasting. But that doesn't do the word justice. A craft is *any* activity that involves making things by hand. It might be drawing, making a collage, threading beads or sculpting with dough; but it might also be constructing an aquarium or train track, or building a castle with wooden blocks or sand. Even cooking is a craft for young kids to enjoy (see page 77).

This gives you plenty of scope as a parent to either acquire some craft skills or bring to the fore some skills that you knew you had or, perhaps, never knew you had. As far as your child is concerned, he will be easily inspired to make things, so long as his hand skills continue to have lots of encouragement. See what craft takes his fancy. Some children love building train tracks or using blocks and large pieces of Lego; others may be happier making things with coloured ribbons and pipe cleaners, pine cones, shells, bits of old fabric, cardboard boxes and cellophane.

Have some boxes handy for storing different kinds of craft materials and try to make them available for your child when he asks for them. If he doesn't show an interest in one of these activities – constructing a train track, for example – put that away for a while and let him focus on other things. Later, he may surprise you by asking for the train-track pieces. And when you bring them down for him it will be like getting a new toy. You can do the same with a box of playdough materials, a box of wooden blocks or any other art and craft materials that you've collected – give it a try, then give it a rest. This process makes for a much less chaotic environment in which to play with your child – and your child will appreciate that too.

Your involvement in any of these activities need only be subtle. Your child will learn best by observing you working on your own creation alongside him, rather than by you trying to take control of his hands. Sometimes he will ask for your assistance and you may need to give him some ideas on how to get started. But try to resist the parental urge to complete your child's creation – to put the eyes in the 'right' spot on an animal he has drawn, in order to 'finish' it. His ideas are likely to be quite different from yours and this is, after all, his creation. With some appealing materials at hand, your subtle encouragement and a little creative freedom, he will just get on with the task of perfecting his work – practising constantly to give his fingers the required skills.

DRAWING IT

Set up, permanently, a little table and chair in the corner of a room so that your child can draw at any time. Have paper, crayons, pencils or whatever is appropriate ready for use. Try to remember to take these drawing implements with you on an outing if there is any possibility you will be kept waiting and need something to entertain your child. Children will put pencil to paper with very little encouragement. They also love whiteboards, 'magic doodle boards' (which allow them to wipe the slate clear) and working with chalk. You could also have a supply of stamps and stickers for him to add to his picture if he feels like it. Try drawing with him to start with; then he is likely to be happy to continue on his own.

You do not have to say much when you are drawing together. But if your child does need ideas for things to draw, try talking to him about what you saw on a recent outing – the trees, flowers, duck pond, children playing. Talk about how you got there – in the car, train or bus, over a bridge or through a tunnel – and what the weather was like. You could also get him started by talking about a recent or upcoming special event. For example:

* *Let's draw a special picture to give your cousin for her birthday. What are some of Anna's favourite things?*
* *Can you paint Holly at her school sports day yesterday? What colour shirt was Holly wearing? Did she have a hat on? Can you remember when she was pulling the long rope?*

Show your interest in his drawings by asking him some questions about them. It doesn't matter if he doesn't want to discuss them. You could also try showing him pictures by other artists in case he is interested in talking about them.

I was surprised to find one four-year-old commenting on a rather challenging collection of abstract art. The child was convinced he could see a dog's face in what appeared to my untrained eye to be no more than a collection of dots and slashes. On closer observation, however, I had to agree with him – and have noticed that dog's face in the painting ever since.

PAINTING IT

Most children aged one to three years will love expressing themselves with a paintbrush in hand. By age four, however, some children will prefer more precision in their drawings, which they can achieve more easily with a texta or a pencil than a paintbrush. Painting will still appeal but you may find they are more interested in covering an object with paint rather than trying to paint a picture. For example, they might like to:

- paint their feet, hands or leaves and make imprints on paper
- paint cardboard boxes to make houses or cardboard rolls to make canoes and boats

One friend, at a bit of a loss as to what to do with her children one afternoon, suggested they paint the driveway while she kicked back and relaxed for a while. She had a great time – oh, and so did the children. Young children love the responsibility involved in completing this sort of task and seeing the grand result. Of course, not all of us have the luxury of being able to offer such an activity to a child, but if you can give them something a bit different to do occasionally – painting a cubbyhouse or an old wooden chair, for example – it may be very appealing and keep them busy for some time.

CONSTRUCTING IT

The first thought for many of us, when constructing something with a young child, is to make something we've bought for them – a train set, for instance, or a Lego farm. As discussed in the previous chapter, children love the precision of certain toys. Puzzles are another example of such a toy and, as well as appealing to a child's natural sense of order, puzzles are also great for refining finger movements.

For some children, though, construction work is often more free form. I bought my son's first train set (with large wooden pieces) when he was one year old. He wasn't thrilled about it and rarely used it. But I persisted and, perhaps to satisfy my own childhood fantasies, I bought him a second train set (with slightly smaller pieces) when he was two. He only really started using the second set when he was five years old. Prior to that, he was happier constructing things in other ways. For example, he would gather together a huge pile of ribbons and pipe-cleaners and use this to make a home for his animals. He loved coloured cellophane, tissue paper, cardboard rolls and some strange grass-like wrapping paper that he found in a newsagent one day.

His favourite materials of all were the real thing – leaves, sticks, sand, stones – and he would sometimes sneak these into the house and add them to one of the animal homes he had built. He soon discovered that, inside, leaves rot and smell, so construction work continued out-side. There he enjoyed making things like farms and aquariums for his small plastic animals. My favourite was his construction of the 'islands of Antarctica'. He filled plastic containers with water, put in a couple of large rocks for islands and used plastic lids for floating icebergs. Ferns were added ('seaweed') as well as twigs and, occasionally, sand. His little hands would then go to great efforts, carefully positioning each Antarctic animal in exactly the right spot on one of the rocks or icebergs, or placing them under the sea. There was always a danger that one of the floating icebergs would sink under the weight of a family of small plastic polar bears; much care and concentration was required to ensure this did not happen.

The point is that it really doesn't matter what materials your child uses for construction purposes, as long as they are safe. And don't be blinded by any preconceived ideas about what materials are good for boys and what are good for girls. Most children – boys and girls – love some kind of construction work, but try to let them experiment with a range of different materials to see what appeals the most. It may be what you least expect.

MOULDING IT

Playdough – that now ubiquitous children's toy. There are many varieties available to buy, or you can make it yourself (look for recipes on the Internet). It is easy to see why little hands can't wait to plunge in. Playdough feels good and is simple for children to control and shape. The only downside is that it apparently tastes good as well. But once your child has stopped trying to eat it, moulding dough can be a very relaxing activity for everyone involved. It is not a particularly messy material to work with: all you need is a plastic tablecloth and a pot of dough (or a few pots of different-coloured dough, if you like).

There is quite a range of playdough accessories available that you may be tempted to buy – plastic moulds, cutters, knives, rolling pins and various other plastic tools for making playdough spaghetti, playdough gardens and the like. The moulds (animals, geometric shapes and so on) can be good but I found most of the other tools quite useless once bits of playdough started to harden on the plastic (I rarely felt inspired to clean it out). The best playdough accessories I found were a small wooden rolling pin, a few different-shaped moulds, and some paddlepop sticks and matchsticks (useful for making hedgehogs, houses, flowers and dinosaurs). See what inspires your child. The simplest of materials can often provide more than enough variation in this activity.

COOKING IT

While most parents I know seem quite willing to mould a worm or two with playdough, cooking with young kids is not always greeted with the same level of enthusiasm. The reasons are obvious enough – it's messy and potentially hazardous (too many hotspots, sharp knives and breakable jugs and bowls). If it is done at all it might be for the occasional special event that requires sweet treats like cupcakes, chocolate crackles or gingerbread men. But with little chance to practise during the intervening periods, small hands start to fumble and what starts out as a happy bonding experience may quickly end in tears.

The better approach, in my experience, is to gradually introduce your child to food preparation and helping out in the kitchen. It is possible to start introducing cooking-related activities to a very young child. A two-year-old will enjoy, for example:

* pouring water or milk from a small jug into a cup or bowl
* sorting dry cereal and sultanas into bowls and 'feeding' them to his toy animals (as in **Feed the animals** on page 131)
* sprinkling grated cheese on pasta or hundreds and thousands on ice-cream (just pour some into a little bowl and let him sprinkle them with his fingers)
* peeling a banana
* feeling the skin of different vegetables and fruits (smooth apple, prickly pineapple and hairy kiwifruit).

By age three you can start to encourage your child to be a little more independent at mealtimes. Make the most of this time when, unlike later, he will not protest about helping out – rather, he will relish the opportunity to do things all by himself. For example:

* He will like the idea of getting his own breakfast. Store his eating utensils at his level so he can get out his own plate and spoon, and make sure that he can reach his cereal. Provide a suitable (small) jug just for him and help him pour his own milk.
* He will happily take his plate from the table and put it by the sink or dishwasher.

* He will like to help make his own sandwich. He could get out the bread and butter from the fridge and start to spread his bread with a safe knife. For a bit of variation, show him how to cut the bread into shapes with pastry cutters. He'll be good at this if he has been using cutters with playdough.

* He can learn to cut up a banana or other soft fruit with a safe knife. Always stay close when he is doing this and keep reminding him to take great care.

* He will enjoy making a pizza with you. Pizzas are easy to prepare. Use small pita-bread or pizza bases and brush them with a pizza topping. Cut up different ingredients – grated cheese, ham, roast capsicum, chicken and olives, for example – and put them into separate little bowls. Let him enjoy choosing what he wants to put on top of his pizza.

When you decide to embark on cooking some sweet treats together, try not to be too ambitious. There is no need, for example, to involve your child in the entire process of baking a cake (unless you go for the easy packet-mix variety). Cake and cookie baking can be quite an undertaking – even for five- and six-year-olds. It's better to ask him to help with a couple of discrete tasks. For example, he may enjoy doing one or two of the following activities:

* breaking the eggs (although messy at first, you will be amazed at how quickly he starts to perfect the required finger movement)
* sifting flour
* pouring liquid into the dry mixture and starting to mix them together
* moulding cookie mixture into round balls and putting them on a baking tray (one or two rows will probably be as many as he'll do)
* smoothing icing on a cake with a spatula and planting the candles.

Inspire the chef

By age four, your child may be ready to create his very own dish. Safely, try to let him experiment with this. Discuss some ideas for making a salad or soup or some sort of healthy pre-dinner snack. See what he tries to concoct. And do make an effort to sample his cooking. There is nothing more disheartening than someone who says no to celery sticks with squished cheese-cube and cracked pepper on top. He will be thrilled to pass them around and see people enjoying them.

Encourage safety

Of course, safety must be foremost in your mind when working with children in the kitchen. Always be with your child in the kitchen as you teach him about:

* cutting with a **sharp** knife or scissors. Always monitor the use of knives and keep sharp knives out of reach.
* being very careful when there is **boiling** water on the stove or **hot** dishes in the oven or microwave. Keep saucepan handles turned inwards on the stove so that they cannot be knocked. When taking things out of the oven to cool, make sure that little hands cannot reach them.
* handling **breakable** dishes. Explain the difference between breakable and unbreakable.

But before paranoia sets in, let me say that it is truly remarkable to watch a young child doing some real work in the kitchen. They do somehow sense the responsibility you are giving them and rise to the challenge sooner than you might expect.

Indulge the senses

Sometimes, let your child smell, taste and feel the food you are cooking. Let him smell jars of dried herbs and spices, break off bits of fresh basil and peel the outer layers of an onion. If you are roasting vegetables, for example, let him mix the olive oil into the vegetables with his fingers. If you are making a quiche, let him trim the edges off the pastry once it is in the tin. Let him knead some dough and watch it rise before baking it.

Encourage him to grow some of his own herbs or vegetables. This really isn't hard. If you don't have a garden, all you need are some pots, soil and packets of seed. To see a four-year-old bursting with excitement as he discovers the first shoots or counts the first tomatoes from the seeds he has sown is well worth the effort.

We will talk more about the joys of indulging a child's senses in the next chapter. But there is no better way to start stimulating his senses than by involving your child in the making of food. All you need to add is a little conversation and you have all the senses activated, just by doing a few things in the kitchen together.

If you need more encouragement . . .

As parents who probably long for such a service, it's often hard to understand why a child isn't excited about having meals presented to him each day as a fait accompli. When they squirm and fuss about eating, it is easy to conclude that our children are 'bad eaters' and to resort to ever more time-consuming methods of hiding the vegetables. More often than not, however, I think children are simply bored eaters rather than bad eaters. Helping them to understand where food comes from and getting them more involved in its preparation can spark an interest that will last a lifetime. They will be encouraged to try different foods. They will become curious about food and start asking you tricky questions like why some eggs are brown and some are white. They will be inspired to create their own little dishes. It may seem daunting; it will be messy at times. But the art and craft of cooking is a tremendous skill. Your child won't need any encouragement to get started on it early – just you.

7. Simple Pleasures
SENSING AND FEELING

And every time he went by, he would begin to walk very, very slowly, and he would hold his nose high in the air and take long deep sniffs of the gorgeous chocolatey smell all around him. Oh, how he loved that smell!

Roald Dahl, CHARLIE AND THE CHOCOLATE FACTORY

Do you love chocolate? Or do you prefer the first bite of a perfectly ripe peach? Do you remember the last time you saw a full moon appear from behind the clouds or a red sun setting over the ocean? Is there a piece of music that will always brighten your mood?

It is easy to forget how new children are to this world – how much they have to experience for the very first time. The simple sensations in life are often the greatest pleasures for them – it might be feeling the wind on their face, looking at the world through a piece of coloured cellophane, feeling a soft silk cushion on their cheek or hearing an interesting bird call. What thrills me as a parent is the ability to experience the wonder of the world all over again, not just through a child's eyes but through all her senses.

One of the miracles of early childhood is the ability to absorb vast amounts of information through the senses – young children literally 'soak up' their environment. Montessori recognised this and spoke of the importance of 'educating' a young child's senses. This might sound obvious but it is surprising how many children miss out on a variety of simple sensory experiences. Babies are often restrained in a pram without so much as a leaf to hold in their hand or a flower to twirl while on their daily 'walk'; toddlers are presented with meals, day-in day-out, without the chance to be involved in their preparation; children are shuffled from one activity to another with no time to pause and observe an ant on the ground or collect stones; electronic entertainment (which they can see and hear but not touch, taste or smell) is turned on and left on for long periods.

Practically, we can't constantly be providing our child with an amazing concoction of sensory stimuli. But it's not difficult to indulge her senses for short periods of time. Once you've started down this path, and witnessed the level of excitement she gains from the simplest of pleasures, you will be hooked.

Start by simply focusing on whatever your child is hearing, seeing or touching at any moment in time – whether at home, or when you are out and about. For example, if I stop typing right now and just focus on what I can hear – I can hear the printer buzzing softly, the clock ticking, a bus going past, a bird chirping, someone mowing a lawn . . . and now there's a plane going overhead as well. Take your child to where the sound is coming from, point to it or compare it with something else she has heard.

Focus on everyday tasting and smelling opportunities as well – onions cooking, coffee brewing, bread baking or fresh strawberries. Don't let these experiences pass by without comment; use colourful words to describe them and to help her remember. Enjoy talking while you walk with your child in a garden, plant nursery or park, and draw her attention to the perfume of roses, jasmine or orange blossom, or the scent of pine cones, eucalyptus, peppermint leaves, cut grass or chopped wood. Maybe you strongly dislike certain smells – the smell of strong cheese, mushrooms, certain farm animals, burning rubber, fish markets or diesel fumes. Whether it's pleasant or unpleasant, the smell sensation evokes a strong reaction that you can talk about with your child.

You may be surprised to see how a child reacts to different sensations. One child I know used to grab pieces of lemon to suck on – something I've never particularly enjoyed. Others have commented on how their child's hearing is much more sensitive than their own. The child may be bothered by noises that are not really loud enough to bother an adult.

Think about past sensory experiences in your life that have left a strong impression. Some people can recall the scratch of chalk on the blackboard from their schooldays; the colour of the wall in the doctor's surgery; the scent of a perfume that reminds them immediately of a specific person; or the cold, clammy feel of a frog they once found.

One friend says she only has to think of the marketplace in Dubai and she can smell the aromatic spices, the cauldrons of curries and the overwhelming sweetness in the air from the bags of cloves, cardamom and nutmeg. For another friend, the smell of cinnamon immediately triggers a memory of her grandmother baking apple cakes. I recall scraping the bowl of my grandmother's homemade soup to reveal a little snow scene imprinted on the plate. And I remember filling my grandfather's pipe with tobacco – and, I admit, liking the smell. It still reminds me of him.

You are building your child's memory through sensory experiences. Endeavour to make these impressions good ones – they may have more impact on her life than you will appreciate at the time. In *The Absorbent Mind* (see Further Reading), Maria Montessori writes:

> *The child does not look at the world as we do. We may see something and say, 'How beautiful!' then go on to other things and retain this vaguely as just a memory. But the child builds his inmost self out of the deeply felt impressions he receives, and this especially in the first part of his life.*

All the activities in this book focus on *combining* sensory stimuli in some way or another – enabling your child to see, hear and touch (while touching and turning the pages of a book as you read together, for example), or to see, hear, smell, taste and touch (as you cook together). The sensory games in Chapter 10 (look for the ⊙☺ symbol) simply aim to indulge your child's senses a little further, encouraging her to recognise differences in colour, shape, texture, sound, taste and smell. By engaging in these activities, not only are you helping to develop her memory, but you are encouraging her to seek out and notice details that a less perceptive person might fail to notice.

As always, these games are only introductory ideas. Once you begin to think about the importance of sensory stimuli, you will find random opportunities throughout your child's day to stimulate her senses, encouraging her to stop in her tracks and enjoy the experience with you.

8. Play it Again

MUSIC AND MOVEMENT

Ah, music. A magic beyond all we do here!

J. K. Rowling, HARRY POTTER AND THE PHILOSOPHER'S STONE

A YOUNG CHILD'S EAR is so receptive that it is as effortless for him to soak up music as it is for him to take in language. Simple, repetitive tunes – particularly if sung by you – help develop his language, aid memory and increase vocabulary. Tunes with a strong beat encourage his sense of rhythm and freedom of movement. Favourite tunes prompt him to make up his own words spontaneously and begin to pitch notes. And, as he gets a bit older, good dancing music and sing-along songs help his social and emotional development as he joins others in singing, dancing and bashing away at percussion instruments.

These more measurable effects of music are easy to write about and no one can doubt their importance. But what of developing a love of music, listening to music for its own sake? The power and pure pleasure of music is beyond words. All I can say from my experience is that your child is lucky if you impart a passion for music when he is young. This doesn't mean you have to be musical or play a musical instrument. If you love music you can just make it part of your day by singing, playing or listening to it with your child. Start this as early as possible. Even a baby will love watching you singing and dancing and feeling the rhythm of the music as you hold him. By the time he can stand on his own two feet, he will be joining in with you.

AN EAR FOR MUSIC

I am always amazed to see the impact certain music has on different children. Some children revel in the noisy, active participation of dancing or banging drums to music; others might just love the comfort and security of a few regular bedtime songs. Some have their obvious favourites from a very early age. Others soon start to distinguish between songs that sound happy or sad.

One child I know would run and find his favourite soft toy whenever he heard 'Puff the Magic Dragon'. No other song would make him do this. Another child was three when he first heard Schubert's song 'The Erlking'. He did not understand the words – they were in German anyway – but sensed that it was a sad song and would say, 'I want to hear the sad song again.' And, from a very young age, one little girl knew immediately when the music meant dance. She felt the beat and she *had* to move!

Every child's response to music is different. Even children from musical families may respond very differently.

Two parents I know, who are both classical musicians, played nursery rhymes on the piano and sang constantly to their babies from day one. When they were listening to CDs in the car, they would always sing along. And yet, their two children responded quite differently. The youngest was always very pitch-oriented and sang all the time. She made up rhymes and turned them into songs. The eldest, on the other hand, was much more rhythmic and could drum nursery rhyme rhythms before he could talk. He'd watch and listen to classical music DVDs all day long, if he could. Then, at age five, he switched to superheros and classical music was put on the backburner. But his parents are sure it is still inside him . . . to be resumed at a later stage.

Don't be surprised if your child wants to listen to certain music and songs over and over again, just like his favourite bedtime story. You may tire of the repetition but he won't.

DANCE

Rhythm comes naturally to many children and is evident as you watch them dancing, clapping hands or bobbing up and down on chubby legs. As they get older you may recognise simple dance movements as they sway in time with the music and imitate older children and adults. If your child loves to move with the beat, put on some dancing music and dance with him. This activity can be as colourful and expressive as you like.

My mother always put a scarf around her head while she was dancing with her grandchildren. This developed into putting a scarf around her waist as well, *and* twirling a scarf in each hand. The kids loved this ritual and, of course, always imitated her. Such an exercise could become a full-blown production with hats and flowers and ribbons as well – but that's up to you.

SONG

If you are not a dancer, at least try to exercise the vocal chords occasionally by singing with your child. When you sing, just make it as natural as when you talk to your child. He wants to listen, to watch your face and mouth and to be near you, especially at bedtime. Don't worry if you think you sing out of tune – your child is not going to hold it against you (although he might develop a preference for the best singer in the house!).

RHYME

If you're *still* telling me you can't sing, then just *say* the words of a song with rhythm in your voice. If you are short of ideas on how to do this, start with some of the old nursery rhymes (see Appendix 3 for ideas). Whether *you* like them or not, young kids love the nonsense words, repetition and word patterns of an old rhyme that has stood the test of time. It is such an easy way to develop their language skills – your child hears the words then delights in repeating them.

Once you have familiarised yourself with the old favourites, try to make up little rhymes of your own. Even the most basic words can become lyrics.

MUSICAL ACTIVITIES

So, now that you have the basics, how can you include some more song and dance into your daily activities with a child? For a start, have at least one CD with children's songs and nursery rhymes. It is a great help to have an accompaniment that is simple and vocals that are very clear so that your child can pick up the words. And have a variety of CDs ready to play in your child's bedroom, the kitchen and the car.

When he is tiny . . .

* rock your baby gently in your arms while you are singing or playing music. As he gets older, you can hold his hands and move them gently in time to the music. By the time he is six months old, you can give him some maracas to shake.
* while he is in the bath, sing songs like 'Five little ducks' (doing actions with your fingers), 'Open, shut them' (as you stretch and curl your fingers), and 'Incy Wincy spider' (doing the actions of climbing up and coming down) – see Appendix 3 for lyrics
* have some of your favourite music ready to play in his room after his bath
* sing softly (a lullaby or something gentle like 'Twinkle twinkle little star', doing some actions with your fingers) when he is ready for bed

As he gets older . . .

* comment on music that might be playing in the house, and help him start to identify the sounds of different instruments (see **The Sounds of Music**, page 123)

* let him watch any live musical performance if you get the opportunity

* encourage him to dance or march with you when you hear suitable music (see **Dance to a Different Beat**, page 112)

* clap out the rhythm as you sing a song (see **Guess What I'm Clapping**, page 172). Show him how to clap his hands like you as you sing, 'If you're happy and you know it, clap your hands'.

* make up a rhythm as you knock on the door, and let him imitate you

* bring out some percussion instruments from time to time and let your child play along with the music. Tambourine, drum, bells, xylophone, maracas, triangles and rhythm sticks are all popular – or you can show him how to use a plastic bowl and a wooden spoon.

* encourage him to sing into a microphone (you could make one out of a cardboard roll and a soft ball, use a toy one, or use a real one if you have one)

* read a book that has an accompanying music CD

* sing two notes and ask him which was higher

* show him what it means to sing softly and loudly then sing two notes and ask him which was louder

* ask your child sometimes, 'Which is your favourite song?'

The musical games in Chapter 10 (look for the 🎵 symbol) include a range of other similar activities so that you can enjoy dancing and moving around with your child if you need an activity on a wet day. Or, if you just want some relaxation time, you could listen to and talk about music together.

We cannot predict how our children will react to music nor whether they will be 'musical'. But regardless of musical ability, anyone can have a passion for music. Marvel at its impact and let it work its magic on your child.

9. The Curious Child
EXPLORING AND DISCOVERING

Said one four-year-old to his pregnant mother:

'How did the baby get into your tummy?'

As his mother dithered about, wondering how best to answer this one, he continued, 'I think you must have eaten lots of eggs and one had a baby inside it.'

He was satisfied with his answer and continued with what he was doing.

YOUNG CHILDREN ARE CONSTANTLY observing what is going on around them, seeking to make connections and understand things. You may not realise the processing going on in their minds, until one day they surprise you with an action or observation that shows their logic at work.

This natural curiosity is apparent from birth. Using all their senses to guide them, babies embark on a relentless quest to investigate everything. And what's most remarkable is that, despite immense frustrations as a result of being unable to control their body movements adequately or to make their wishes known without the power of language, *they keep on trying*. They can't help themselves – they are too curious about the world to let either distress or injury dissuade them, and too desperate for independence to give up.

While the frustrations diminish with increasing control, independence and knowledge, young children's innate desire to investigate remains strong. By age three, armed with language and a very basic understanding of the world, they seek new kinds of encouragement to satisfy their curiosity.

QUESTIONS AND SUGGESTIONS . . .

One of the simplest ways to stimulate a young child's curiosity is to ask her questions. You can start by focusing on things in her daily world, either in the familiar environment of the home or while you are out and about together. There are so many simple things you can discuss with her. Keep reminding yourself that you are in the unique position of being able to make her think about certain things for the very first time. For example, you could ask her:

* *Where does the water go when you pull out the bath plug?*
* *Where do you think the olives in this jar came from?*
* *Where do the birds sleep at night?*
* *What made those marks on the tree trunk?*
* *What will happen if we leave this plastic bag on the beach?*
* *How can that tiny ant carry such a big leaf?*

❋ *Why do the leaves fall off the trees in winter?*

You could also talk about an everyday problem or task and discuss a possible solution or way of carrying it out. For example:

❋ *This shopping bag is too heavy for me to carry. How will we get the shopping up the stairs?*
❋ *It's very hot now. What do you think we should do to cool down?*
❋ *This tap is too high for you to reach. What can we do to make it easy for you to reach the tap?*
❋ *How should we wrap this present for Mum?*
❋ *How can we clean up all these little rice bubbles?*

As she gets more familiar with your questions, you could ask her about hypothetical situations, too. For example:

❋ *How could you build a house if you didn't have bricks?*
❋ *How could you tell Dad you were hungry if you couldn't use words?*
❋ *What else could we use this sock for?*
❋ *How could we get to the other side of a river if there wasn't a bridge?*

There is no need to bombard her with questions, but ask one or two when the opportunity presents itself. And make sure your own interest in the topic is apparent. Your child will love the fact that you are engaging her in discussion and making her feel important. You will get some fantastic answers! The idea is not to see whether she answers correctly or even sensibly, but to set her mind ticking over, to develop her understanding of people and the environment, and to encourage her imagination – and her sense of humour.

Taking your lead, she will gradually start to ask more questions herself. That does not mean we must have all the answers. Most parents find it hard to gear answers to a level that is age-appropriate. But in these early years, you often don't have to say very much – the simpler the response, the better. Try asking your child what they think, and taking your response from there. And before you twist yourself in knots trying to think of the 'correct' answer, keep in mind that not every response has to be dead serious – there is a place for some light-hearted answers and a bit of nonsense, too.

. . . AND INVENTIONS

Another simple way of stimulating a child's natural curiosity is to suggest she invents something. Children are experts at creating things out of whatever they've got in front of them. (A piece of string and a bottle top might make an excellent stethoscope, for example; they don't need the real thing or even a toy version.) Necessity is also the mother of children's inventions and they will prove this to you in all sorts of weird and wonderful ways.

One resourceful three-year-old, desperate to play in a school band alongside his brother and sister, invented his own instrument to take on the stage. It was a toy crane, shaped a bit like a saxophone, and he called it his cranophone.

By suggesting she invents something, you are simply building on what comes to your child quite naturally. Choose something she likes. If she likes dressing up, you might suggest she invents a new hat. If she likes animals, she might invent a new kind of animal. If she likes music, she might invent a new kind of musical instrument. Encourage her to draw it or make it out of some materials you have to hand. Give it a name. Ask lots of questions about it. The more you ask questions, the more she'll be encouraged to think about her invention and what it does.

DON'T MISS THE MAGIC OF NATURE

From a very early age, some children have a special affinity with nature. They are totally at ease pottering around in a garden or park. They love using sticks in the dirt, collecting little seeds that have dropped from a tree, or even just lying back in some soft grass. They are protective of ants and bugs. They will warn you to be careful where you tread. They won't let you disturb a spider's web and will notice particular flowers and leaves.

You can encourage this characteristic in many ways – most of all by getting out and about with your child and giving her some freedom to explore. See what captures her attention, even fleetingly, and show your interest in something she has seen, heard, smelt or felt. Here are just a few ideas:

* Look at leaves blowing in the wind. Let her feel the wind on her face.
* Lie on the grass and watch the clouds. See what shapes you can find in the clouds together. See what she thinks might be 'in the clouds'.
* Talk about the sun and explain that it always comes up in the east and goes down in the west. When it is sunny, look for shadows and point out her shadow.

* Make a point of looking for the full moon each month. Talk about the moon rising and the stars appearing.
* Go out of your way to see a sunset sometimes, at the right time and place. Talk about the colour changes in the sky and why the sun disappears at night.
* Go exploring in a garden or park – take a magnifying glass.
* Go exploring at night – take a torch.
* Look at stones and shells and discuss their different weights, shapes, colours and textures.
* Let her help you plant little flowers or vegetables in the garden or in pots (see page 81).
* Pick up petals or flowers on the ground. Put them in a circle on the grass like a magic fairy ring so that the fairies will come to your garden that night.
* Spot birds' nests and other animal homes. Discuss where a snail might be heading and what it is going to eat. If you are at the beach, go and explore the rockpools – see if you can find any 'moving shells'.
* Make a 'fish pond' or 'frog pond' at home – your child will love to construct a home for these animals using water, leaves and stones (even if the animals themselves are not the real thing!).
* Talk about why we need water and ways to save it. Talk about where it can be found (oceans, ponds, snow, hail, taps, drains . . .); all the things it can do (freeze, evaporate, squirt, dribble . . .); and what it can look like (crystal-clear, dirty, coloured, bubbly . . .). Watch the rain and discuss where the water goes. Talk about floods and droughts and how precious water is. Children are fascinated by it.

My mother still recalls her then three-year-old son's first experience with hail. He was running around in the rain outside, getting soaking wet and loving it. Suddenly, he stopped in his tracks, then came running inside, breathless and shouting, 'There's something coming down with the rain!'

CURIOSITY BUILT THE CHILD

With *freedom* to explore, *time* to observe and our gentle guidance and *encouragement*, a child's natural curiosity will develop into an ability to wonder at the world. This is an incredible development in a young child's life – although not one that you will read about very often. It's difficult to pinpoint exactly when it happens, but if you are looking for it, you will notice a gradual change in your child's nature. She will show a growing sense of love and care for the environment, and will naturally start to do things to protect it. She will start to take more care around the house and with things entrusted to her. She will show a deeper interest in why things happen and how things work. She will display a greater sense of independence. You will frequently find her engrossed in her own creative endeavours, happily 'playing' alone.

At this stage, a young child has absorbed so much of what is going on around her and is curious to discover so much more. It's fascinating to watch this as a parent or carer – and most gratifying to feel that you've played a part.

10. Playtime
THE GAMES

THIS CHAPTER OFFERS step-by-step instructions on how to play simple games with children aged one to five years. The symbol beside each game indicates which play theme from the previous chapters is featured.

For activities to use with babies, and ideas for grandparents who live far away from their grandchildren, see Appendixes 1 and 2.

Here are some tips on how to play the games:

KNOW YOUR CHILD

Even at age four, your child may only be interested in a single activity for a few minutes. You will know when he's had enough. The minute he starts to lose interest and wriggle around, stop playing. A child must *want* to come back for more.

On the other hand, if you have captured his attention and your child is really enjoying a game, continue playing, if you can. Observe how he responds – he may have some new ideas himself. If he really likes a certain game, keep adapting it as he gets older to make it more challenging.

START SIMPLY

You will need to help your child when you play a game for the first time. He will follow your lead to get the idea. Suggestions for what you might say to your child are given in italics; these words make it easy for him to understand, and make the game sound fun. The main thing is to make your child feel comfortable, as well as engaged, when you're playing with him. Don't try to make things too challenging at the beginning; you can always move onto a slightly harder version of the same game later.

WORK AROUND THEIR ROUTINE

You don't need to stimulate your child constantly with games and activities. If he is playing happily by himself, try not to interrupt him – wait until a diversion is needed.

Most children have a natural rhythm to their day: they get dressed, they get ready to go out, they spend time outside the house, they come home, they have a bath, they have a meal, then it's bedtime – or something similar.

As discussed in Chapter 1, these regular events and activities provide an excellent framework around which to build playtime. By incorporating a few games into your child's daily routine, you'll find that you can give new life to sometimes tedious activities. If, for instance, a child knows that when he has a bath there'll be a chance to play 'the animal-guessing game', he'll look forward to bathtime more. And you will end up damp but laughing and hugging after his bath. Look for the 🕐 symbol for similar ideas.

TAKE THE TIME TO PREPARE

The games are designed to require minimal preparation. Sometimes, though, just two minutes' preparation will be invaluable if it means that your child doesn't get distracted or lose interest in the middle of an activity. For instance, if you're cooking together, have the ingredients and utensils laid out beforehand. This will mean you don't have to interrupt the flow by looking for the flour or a cup measure.

Most of the props that are recommended – whether it be toy animals or scarves or plastic buckets – you will have around the house.

COMMUNICATE AT THEIR LEVEL

Children love to feel close to those around them, so when possible, get down on the floor – or the bed or the lounge – with your child when you're talking to him. Maintain eye contact and try to give him your full attention for your short time together.

PLAY IT AGAIN

You'll be amazed how some young children will want you to repeat a certain game time after time. Indulge them – as discussed on page 9, there is no need for too much variety. By performing an activity again and again, they will be practising new skills.

LET THEM PLAY THE ADULT

Children love the idea of being the adult so let them, occasionally. All the games start with you explaining what will happen, but as your child gets older and more familiar with the games, you will be able to swap roles so that he gives the instructions. (Where this is possible, it is indicated under 'Variations'.) You may hear him imitating you exactly as he explains how the game will work.

BE REALISTIC

When you first play a game, it may seem that your child doesn't understand it at all. Don't be discouraged. Your child may remember something of it, he may not, but as you repeat it, certain things will start to become familiar to him. Before too long, you may find him anticipating what comes next, getting great pleasure out of listening to you act out the scenario, and even giving instructions himself.

Don't be too hard on yourself. Remember that it will get easier, especially as your confidence grows.

AGE GUIDES

The games are arranged in age order but, as discussed earlier (see page 14), the age recommendations beside each game are only guides. You will soon see how many of the games can be modified to suit different age groups so you can involve children of different ages in the same game. For example:

Shops (page 168)

A three-year-old could play a very simple version of this game with a toy cash register and two or three toys to sell. Your five-year-old, meanwhile, will still love playing shops, but by now he will decide on what to sell (vegetables, toys, cushions or artworks, perhaps), sort these things into piles by himself and even decide how much each thing costs.

Playhouse (page 143)

A two-year-old will enjoy just walking in and out of a playhouse, perhaps with a few soft toys. Four- and five-year-olds will think of many more interesting things to do as they build the 'house' and then decorate and furnish it.

Treasure hunt (page 159)

You can use easy verbal clues for a two-year-old. For a four-year-old, you can write clues on paper and read them to him.

WHO IS THIS?

Aim

To help your child to learn about herself and people with whom she is familiar. This is an ideal game to play when she is in the bath.

Props

One of her favourite bath toys – perhaps a rubber duck

Play

Focus her attention on the duck. Say:

Who is this? This is Duck. Duck. Hello Duck!

Ask her the question and give her the answer to begin with. Encourage her to say it and then repeat it a couple of times. Then leave it until the next day, when you might say:

Who is this? [touching her tummy] *This is Sophie. Sophie. Hello Sophie!*

Variation

Over the next year, start to tell her other things about herself and her family – just one at a time. Think about ways of making these discussions more appealing. For example, children are often quickly distracted and highly amused if you talk to them through one of their toy animals – especially if you liven it up with an interesting accent.

So, her toy duck might say to her:

Hello, I am Duck. What's your name?

Or Duck might ask:

Where is Sophie's arm?

Where is Sophie's nose?

Where is Sophie's cot?

Experiment with other playful ways of getting the message across. As she gets older you can follow a similar format to slowly teach her:

* her full name
* her age
* her birthday
* which country she lives in
* where other members of her extended family live
* her address

HEAD AND SHOULDERS, KNEES AND TOES

Aim
To help your child learn the names of the parts of the body. Try this while he is in the bath or as you are getting him dry.

Props
You and your child

Play
This is your head [rub his head]. *This is your head. We are drying your head.*
   Head.
This is your arm [rub his arm]. *This is your arm. We are drying your arm.*
   Arm.
Gradually introduce different parts of the body – one at a time.

Variation

Continue to focus on the parts of the body he has learnt so far. But instead of saying *This is your head*, say *Touch your head!* or *Where is your head?* Vary the idea again by swapping roles:

This is Mama's head! [point to your head]

Where is Mama's head? [teach him to touch or point to your head]

More . . .

There are many songs you can use to reinforce the names of parts of the body, for example:

* 'Head and shoulders, knees and toes'
* 'The Hokey Pokey'

WHAT ARE WE WEARING TODAY?

Aim

To encourage your child to learn the names of her clothes. Play this game while you're getting her dressed.

Props

Your child's clothes – have these ready in a pile beside you

Play

Talk to your child as you put on each article of clothing. Explain what you're doing when you're dressing or undressing her. Talk about each article and tell her what it is called.

This is your T-shirt. We are putting on your T-shirt.

These are your jeans. We are putting on your jeans. Right leg in the jeans. Left leg in the jeans. Stand up. Pull up the jeans.

Variations

Make up a simple rhyme as you teach her the names of the clothes she is wearing. For example, you could sing the following words to the tune of 'London Bridge is falling down':

Pull my T-shirt over my head, over my head, over my head,

Pull my T-shirt over my head

Look at me! [or use your child's name]

Or:

I can put my jeans on now, jeans on now, jeans on now

I can put my jeans on now

Look at me!

Or:

First my socks and then my shoes, then my shoes, then my shoes

First my socks and then my shoes

Look at me!

More . . .

Other good tunes you can make up your own words to include:

* 'Old MacDonald had a farm'
* 'Skip to my Lou'
* 'The wheels on the bus'
* 'Do you know the muffin man?'
* 'If you're happy and you know it'

* 'The farmer in the dell'
* 'Here we go round the mulberry bush'

WHERE IS THE GREEN FISH?

Aim

To stimulate the visual sense by focusing on colour.

Props

Toys in bright colours – for example, coloured plastic rings on a pole, barrels, blocks, boats, cars or fish. In this example, we use fish.

Play

While your child is having a bath, line up the coloured fish on the edge. Point to one at a time and tell him what colour it is. Then say:

This is a green fish. [Hold it in front of him.] *Green.* [Hand it to him.] *This fish is green. Can you put the green fish in the water?*

Now we'll put the other fish in the water too. In they go! But where is the green fish? Can you point to the green fish? Green. [Help him at first.] *Well done!* [Mix up the fish in the water.]

Where is the green fish now? Find the green fish. [Help him if necessary.] *Yes, there it is. Well done!*

Vary the language but emphasise only one colour for a few days, until you think your child is ready for a change. When he starts to recognise the colours easily, you can play with them all at once.

Variations

Through repetition of this kind of routine in a variety of situations – in the bath, in the kitchen or wherever suits you best – you can introduce your child to many colours. For example:

While your child is waiting for a meal, you can talk about whatever food you are using that day and show it to her:

This is broccoli. The broccoli is green. Or:

Here is an apple. This apple is red. Or:

Here is a carrot. What colour is the carrot? The carrot is orange.

Vary the routine by asking your child to put fruit or vegetables, one at a time, into a container beside her on the table:

Please put the broccoli into the container. What colour is the broccoli?

Please put the apple into the container. What colour is the apple?

Show your child a red toy and take her to something else in the room that is red.

Use two sets of crayons: hold up a blue crayon and ask your child to find another blue crayon in the second set.

Sort coloured toys or shapes or fruit and vegetables into piles of the same colour.

Use a puzzle with four to six large and different-coloured pieces: help your child to pick out the different-coloured pieces and then put them back again.

Talk about colours while hanging up or sorting out the washing. If you have coloured pegs, say:

Where is the red peg? Can you give me a red peg, please?

Cut out some small pieces of different coloured cellophane and encourage your child to look through them.

Note Do not expect learning colours to happen quickly – depending on what age you start, it may take months for your child to learn just a few. As with all the games, keep the sessions short and when he starts to lose interest, stop. You are always in the best position to gauge how much your child is ready for.

AGES 2+

DANCE TO A DIFFERENT BEAT

Aim

To encourage children to express themselves physically and to 'feel the rhythm'. Most young children love to dance *and* to watch you dancing.

Props

Your favourite songs for dancing

Play

Make a space somewhere in the room, start the music, and dance! Offer some words of encouragement if needed, but the best way to encourage your child is to let go of any inhibitions and dance yourself.

Variations

Wear dress-ups while you dance together – for example, a hat, a skirt to twirl in or scarves to wear and wave around.

As your child gets older, experiment with different kinds of movement, using different kinds of music. For example, use some marching music (like the theme for *Raiders of the Lost Ark*) to march in and out of rooms or around a table. See whether your child can hear the defined marching rhythm and if he can keep time with the beat as he walks around. Or you could use a recording of some sounds from nature (these are readily available, with or without music alongside them) and encourage your child to move like a river or like the wind.

THREE SPOONS IN THE BOX

Aim

To encourage your child to count by touching objects and saying the numbers out loud.

Props

Three spoons
A box

Play

While she is waiting for a meal, put the spoons and the box on the table. Let her play with them first. Pick the spoons up one at a time, saying the numbers *one, two, three* as you put each spoon into the box. Take them out of the box again. Help your child to pick them up one at a time.
How many spoons are here? Let's count them. [Pick up the first spoon.]

One. [Put it in the box. Pick up the next spoon.]

Two. [Put the second spoon in the box with the first one.]

Three. [Put the third spoon in the box.]

Look – there are three spoons in the box. (Take them out again.)

Now it is your turn. Let's count the spoons. [As she picks up the first spoon, say *one* with her and put the spoon in the box. As she picks up the second spoon, say *two* and so on.]

Look – there are three spoons in the box. Good work! Well done!

Variations

When she can do this easily, try counting five spoons.

Using the same ideas, count out plastic animals as you hand them to her in the bath.

Gradually introduce the concept of 'more'. For example, as you add another spoon, say:

Here's one more spoon.

WHAT DAY IS IT TODAY?

Aim

To encourage your child to learn the days of the week as you discuss his regular activities – perhaps while your child is waiting for breakfast.

Props

A big calendar – you can buy or make a calendar or chart that appeals to a young child. Make sure it is easily visible to the child from the breakfast table.

Play

Point out the name of the day on the calendar to reinforce the sequence of days of the week.

What day is it today? It is Monday. Today is Monday. Tom is going to swimming [to the library/to visit his grandparents/to kinder] today.

Variations

* Have paper and pencils ready for him to draw a picture of what might happen today.
* Discuss the weather:

   What is the weather like today? Look! There are clouds in the sky today. Do you think it is going to rain?
* Talk about the seasons:

   It is autumn now. See, the tree out there is losing its leaves. The leaves on the ground make a crunchy noise when you walk on them.

   Or:

   It's cold today. Do you feel cold? You need to wear your jacket. It's winter time now. See, there are no leaves on our tree. They've all gone.
* Talk about festivities and special days celebrated at home or at pre-school and show him things relevant to these.

Note It takes a long time for children to begin to understand the concept of time. By age four, however, they will start to understand things like how long they need to wait until 'next week', how many more nights' sleep until their uncle comes to visit, how many months until their birthday, what Dad means by 'five more minutes' in the playground, what time they go to preschool. At this stage you can start to teach:

* the time – o'clock and half-past
* the date – use the calendar to point to the relevant number in the month
* the names of the months – use the calendar to show him the sequence of the months

MOVE DOG AROUND THE BOX

Aim
To encourage your child to listen to and remember 'little' words, to follow directions and develop her fine-motor skills.

Props
A small toy animal (perhaps a little dog)
A see-through plastic container

Play
Can you please put Dog IN the box? Put him in the box. [Help your child to put dog in the box.]
Dog is in the box. Good. Well done!
Can you please put Dog BEHIND the box? Put him behind the box. [Help your

child until she can follow your instructions on her own.]

Dog is behind the box. Good. Well done!

Can you please put Dog IN FRONT OF the box? Put him in front of the box. Dog
   is in front of the box. Good. Well done!

Gradually add:

Can you please put Dog BESIDE the box?

Can you please help Dog jump OVER the box?

Can you please help Dog walk all the way AROUND the box?

Can you please put Dog UNDER the box?

Variations

Place dog beside the box, then ask your child:

Where is Dog?

This time she has to answer:

BESIDE the box.

Gradually continue in the same way, using all the other descriptions of where the Dog can move.

You can also ask your child to take part physically in the game, asking her, for example, to:

stand BESIDE the table

stand BEHIND the table

walk AROUND the table

get UNDER the table

GOODNIGHT

Aim

To encourage your child to talk and to use familiar words through role play – in this case, putting his toy animals to bed. This boosts his self-esteem by letting him be in charge of a situation instead of having someone else telling him what to do. Talk quietly and slowly as you go through this routine – and enjoy the change of voice and slower pace.

Props

Your child's favourite soft toys or animal friends.

Enough squares of material (tea towels, hand towels, handkerchiefs etc.) to use as 'blankets' for the toys.

Play

We are going to put the animals to bed. It's bedtime for the animals.

[Pick up Little Dog.] *It's bedtime, Little Dog. Did you have a good day today? Are you very tired? Have you brushed your teeth? I hope you have a good sleep. Goodnight, Little Dog.* [Rock Little Dog in your arms, put him down on the bed, pat him and cover him with a blanket.]

[Pick up Big Bear.] *It's bedtime, Big Bear. Did you have a good day today? Are you very tired? Have you brushed your teeth? I hope you have a good sleep. Goodnight, Big Bear.* [Rock Big Bear in your arms, put him down on the bed, pat him and cover him with a blanket.]

[Pick up Peter Rabbit . . .]

Use the same routine with each toy until your child gets the idea – then encourage him to put the animals to bed himself.

Variations

Most families have bedtime 'rituals' for their children. It might be singing a song, saying a poem, tucking them in or giving them a special hug as you put them to bed. Use whatever bedtime routine is familiar to your child as you act out this scene with him and his toys.

TASTE AND SMELL

Aim

To help a young child start to recognise different foods by testing small samples. As well as learning the names of different foods, your child will learn to recognise basic flavours (sweet, sour, salty, spicy) and smells. As discussed in Chapter 6, there is no better way to stimulate all your child's senses than by involving her in the making of food. Food sensations and kitchen conversations about types of food, where food comes from and food preparation can leave an indelible impression on your child – make it a good one.

Props

Choose four different food sensations to start with, from things you have on hand, such as: sugar, chocolate, honey, mild soy sauce, lemon, strawberry, salt, pineapple, red onion, cinnamon, vanilla, mint, seedless olives, apricot, orange, pineapple. Even if she has tasted some or all of the foods before, use this game to help reinforce names and flavours and make comparisons from one flavour to another.

Play

Place four bowls, four little spoons and four different types of food in front of your child at the table. For example, you could set up a jar of honey, a quarter of lemon, some cinnamon and a jar of seedless olives. Sit down at the table with your child. Emphasise that this game only involves a tiny taste.

Let's try the honey first. Smell it. [Hold the jar close to her.] *What does it smell like? Do you like that smell? We will put a little honey on a spoon. Would you like to try it and tell me what it tastes like?* [Let her try it either by herself or with you holding the spoon.] *It is sweet.*

Now we'll try the lemon. Smell it. [Let her handle it as she smells it.] *What does it smell like? Do you want to taste a little bit? You know it is going to be sour, but just put your tongue on it. What did you think? Is it sour and bitter?*

Now let's try the cinnamon. Smell it. [Hold the container close to her.] *Put a little cinnamon on a spoon. Would you like to try it and tell me what it tastes like?* [Help her.] *It is spicy.*

Now let's smell the olives. Is that a strong smell? If I put a little piece of olive on a spoon, would you like to try it and tell me what it tastes like? [Help her.] *It is salty.*

Variations

After you've done some tasting, you could make something to eat. Let her mix up half a teaspoon of cinnamon and half a teaspoon of sugar and sprinkle it on some buttered toast. Put the olives on some pizzas. Squeeze the lemon, add water and a little sugar to taste and make a lemon drink or lemonade iceblocks. This game can be incorporated into lots of other kitchen activities with your child.

Once your child becomes more familiar with this game you can encourage her to test the *smell* of mint, rosemary, basil, nutmeg, cloves, liquorice, onion, garlic, fish, vanilla and lavender. Encourage her to guess the smell of herbs and spices you store in jars at home or things you grow in your garden.

AS STILL AS A STATUE

Aim

To encourage your child to enjoy listening to music and to concentrate on when the music stops.

Props

Music that you like and that is good for dancing.

Play

Clear a space in the room and get the music ready to play. Explain the game to your child:

Do you know what a statue is? [Explain that a statue is usually made of stone and doesn't move – demonstrate by pretending to be a statue.] *We are going to play some music and we are both going to dance. You have to listen carefully and concentrate very hard because when I stop the music you have to stop dancing and pretend to be a statue. You can't move anything. You have to stay still like a statue.* [Demonstrate again, and try to look different to last time so that she gets the idea.] *And you have to stay like that until I start the music again. Now, let's start dancing.* [Start the music and begin dancing. When you decide to stop the music, stop dancing and stay still so that you look like a statue. Your child may begin to imitate you. When you're ready, start the music again and dance. Your child may enjoy finding herself – and you – stopped in funny positions. As she gets older, she will use her imagination more and come up with different ways of being a statue.]

AGES
2+

HELPING OUT AT HOME

Young children generally like to help out at home. Small, regular tasks help to establish a routine for your child; they also make him feel more independent and involved in the things that adults do. Start with simple things like:

* taking his plate and cup to the sink/dishwasher after a meal
* pushing his chair in after he leaves the table
* putting his shoes away in the cupboard
* washing his hands after playing outside
* picking up his clothes after changing into pyjamas and putting them in the dirty-clothes basket
* packing up the bath toys after a bath

As he gets older, involve him in more complex tasks like:

* setting the table for dinner
* helping with the cooking (see Chapter 6)
* watering plants, arranging flowers

✱ helping to cultivate a herb garden or create a vegetable patch

Discussing the tasks to be done provides an excellent opportunity for language development.

THE SOUNDS OF MUSIC

Aim
To encourage your child to listen carefully to particular music and to recognise the sounds of different instruments.

Props
Music you like – with different instruments playing solos.

Pictures of a trumpet, a violin, a flute, a saxophone and a piano (or show him the real thing if you have one in the house).

Play
You can put the music on at any time – perhaps when your child sits down for a meal. Choose one instrument that your child might hear, talk about it, and show him a picture:

We are going to listen to some music. We will have to be quiet while the music is playing to see whether we can hear the trumpet [for example].

Point out the trumpet when you can identify it.

That is the trumpet. Can you hear the trumpet?

Another time:

That is the violin. Can you hear the violin?

That is the saxophone. Can you hear the saxophone?

OPPOSITES

Aim

To introduce your child to the concept of opposites.

Props

Two pieces of string – one long, one short

Two toy animals – one big, one little

Two books – one heavy, one light

Play

Place the three sets of items on the table in front of your child. Start very simply and concentrate on learning one concept first. The opposite will then be easier to understand.

Look at these animals. One of these animals is BIG. Let's pick up the BIG animal. [Help him to choose the big animal.]

Look at this string. One piece of string is LONG. Let's pick up the long piece of string.

Look at these books. One of these books is HEAVY. Let's pick up the heavy book.

Follow this idea for a few times, then introduce the opposite and say, for example:

Look at these animals. One of these animals is BIG. Let's pick up the big animal. [Wait for him to pick up the big animal.] *And one of the animals is LITTLE. Let's pick up the little animal.*

Variations

The opposites below can be explained gradually (one or two at a time), with some appropriate props:

* back and front – toy
* open and shut – box with a lid
* big and small – ball
* in and out – of a box
* on and off – light switch
* loud and soft – talking
* full and empty – cup of milk
* fast and slow – toy animal walking along the table
* happy and sad – facial expressions
* beginning and end – use a book
* stop and go – hold hands and run together, then stop
* awake and asleep – facial expressions/body language
* clean and dirty – compare T-shirts, hands, plates or shoes
* up and down – hand movements
* hot and cold – running the bath
* weak and strong – as you lift your child
* night and day – as it gets dark
* black and white – colours of your clothes
* dark and light – find the darkest place in the house, then the lightest
* warm and cool – find the warmest place in the house, then the coolest

There are also many well-illustrated books available that concentrate on learning opposites.

THIS GOES WITH THAT

Aim

To introduce your child to things that go together and the concept of matching.

Props

A few pairs of items that you have on hand, for example:

* pencil and paper
* bread and butter
* toothpaste and toothbrush
* cup and saucer
* bowl and spoon
* socks and shoes
* clothing tops and bottoms
* bat and ball
* flowers and vase

You can also buy cards and other games with pictures of things that go together. You could use these for a change if you like.

Play

Choose only two pairs of items to start with – for example, pencil and paper, spoon and bowl. Muddle them on the table in front of your child. Say:

We are going to play a game. We are going to work out which things go together.

This is a bowl. We put our food in this bowl and we eat it with a spoon. So, bowl and spoon go together.

This is a pencil. We draw with a pencil. When we draw, we need a piece of paper. So, pencil and paper go together.

As your child begins to understand the concept, muddle more pairs of items on the table for her to match.

Variations

Talk about matching and sorting as you go about daily activities. We do plenty of sorting and matching ourselves around the house but we don't think to talk about it with our child. For example:

* clothes – show your child what you're doing as you match piles of jeans, socks and T-shirts
* toys – talk about what you're doing as you sort toys into piles of soft toys, cars and books
* cutlery – ask your child to help put away the spoons here and the forks there

LET'S PLAY . . . TRAINS

Aim

To expand your child's vocabulary while he's playing with one of his favourite toys – dinosaurs, cars, dolls; in this example, we use trains.

Props

A train and train track

Cars to line up at the crossing

Plastic trees and bushes

Farm animals

Small toy people

Play

The joy of this activity is in the building – take as long as your child likes and talk about what you are building together. Help him to put the track together on the floor or a big table; to build a platform; to 'plant' the trees and bushes; to place groups of animals in fields near the track; to line up cars waiting to go through the crossing after the train has gone past; and to set the train on the tracks. Then talk to him about the scenario:

Here comes the train now. The cars are waiting for it to go through the crossing? Who is waiting on the platform to catch the train? Where will they go?...

See if any specific interest evolves and run with it!

Variations

✳ Set up the train track for a trip across the city instead of the countryside. Build houses, apartment blocks and office blocks. Set up shops, cafes, cars and buses.

✸ For older children, increase the number of tracks, blocks and animals. You will, of course, be able to have a much more complex conversation about the scenario with an older child.

PARTY TIME!

Aim

To nurture your child's love of fanciful characters through role play. She will learn new words and repeat them. This game should also give you another chance to help her practise good manners and be kind to her guests. It boosts her self esteem because she is organising her toys to come to her party – and everyone loves a party.

Props

Building blocks
Some of your child's favourite soft toys
A toy bus or big car
A birthday cake (pretend)
Plastic plates and cups

Play

Together with your child, use the blocks to build a big 'house' for the soft toys, who will be the party guests. Build another house for your child to use on the other side of the room. It may be simply a square outline, as it needs to be large enough to accommodate her and her guests. Both houses should have a front door. The bus driver can pretend to knock on these. Build a road between the houses using whatever is at hand (blocks, straws etc.). Spread out some plates and cups on the floor in your child's house.

Let's pretend we are going to have a party for your birthday. We are going to have a birthday party at your house. [Ask your child to sit on the floor in her house, ready to receive her guests.]

You tell me which friends you want to invite. I will be the bus driver. Here is the bus. I will go and pick up your friends from their house and bring them to your party, one at a time. Now, who are you going to invite first? [Your child will suggest someone. If not, help her to get started – for example, Rabbit.]

Okay, I'll go and get Rabbit. [Pretend to drive the bus to the animals' house and knock at the front door. Use a special voice for the bus driver.] *Knock, knock! Hello. Is Rabbit there? Hello, Rabbit. Would you like to come to Isabel's birthday party?*

Oh, yes please! [Use a different voice for Rabbit.]

Good [bus driver's voice]. *Well, get in the bus. We are going to Isabel's house. Off we go!*

[Drive the bus back to your child's house and knock at her front door.]

Knock, knock!. Hello, Isabel. It's Rabbit here. Can I come in please? Can I come to your party?

Yes. Come in, Rabbit. [Help your child to organise a place for Rabbit to sit on the floor beside her, and pretend to offer her a drink and some cake.]

Continue in this manner until there are enough guests at the party.

Variation

Pretend that one of the animals (Little Dog) cannot come to the party. As you answer the door, say:

*I am so sad. I am coughing too much. I am too sick to come to your party today
(cough cough).*

[Bus driver] *Poor Little Dog. I am sorry you are sick. I hope you get better soon.*

FEED THE ANIMALS

Aim

To develop your child's love of role play, her confidence and imagination as
you create a farm and feed the animals.

Props

Building blocks
Plastic farm animals
Small plastic bowls or plates
Pretend food such as grass, straw, leaves or crumpled-up crepe paper

Play

Help your child to build a farm with the blocks, creating separate pens for
each of the animal groups (pigs, cows, chickens, horses). Put some food
into the bowls or plates and then put these in the pens for the animals.
Talk to the animals as you get their food ready. Speak slowly and use as
much repetition as possible.

Okay, Lucy. Now we are going to feed the animals. [Move to the pigs' pen
using your fingers to 'walk'.] *Hello pigs. Are you hungry? I have some*

scraps for you. Would you like some scraps? [Leave a bowl of food in the pig pen and walk on to the next pen.]

Hello, horses. Are you hungry? I have some hay for you. Would you like some hay?

Oooh, I can hear the cows mooing for their food. They must be hungry! We're coming soon, cows.

Hello, cows. Are you hungry? I have some grass for you. Would you like some grass?

Variations

As you help her learn the names of the animals, tell her about some of their specific characteristics:

Where do we get eggs from? The hens lay eggs. We can collect the eggs from the hen house.

Where do we get wool? The sheep have wool on their backs. We can shear the wool off their backs and make it into warm clothes.

Where do we get milk? We milk the cows to get milk.

You could discuss which food each animal really likes to eat – chickens and pigs eat scraps, cows and sheep eat grass, horses eat hay and so on.

AGES
2½+

DRESS-UPS

Have a box of dressing-up clothes ready for use at any time. Collect old clothes, hats, scarves, fabric remnants, gloves, feathers, belts, masks, shoes and bags. Dress up as a doctor, nurse, astronaut, prince or princess.

Pretend to be a dragon, knight, pirate, fairy, ghost, witch, snowman, kangaroo or tennis player. Whatever your child chooses to be, go along with the appropriate language and behaviour. Simple ideas are better for a younger child (e.g. bus driver or someone/something else he may have seen in real life or his favourite book). As he gets older, you may notice he is imitating characters in books, television shows or movies, or other people he knows or has seen.

LISTENING FOR LETTERS

Aim
To encourage your child to listen carefully for the first letter of a word. Use the Sound Chart on page 43 to pronounce the letters of the alphabet in a way that is easy to start with.

Props
Toys (might include soft toys and small plastic animals, cars, bus, train, boat)
A book
A pencil and paper
Pieces of fruit

Play
Place toys around the room or on a table where your child can see them.

Sit down together. Choose a letter, making sure there are at least two things in the room that start with the sound of that letter. For example:

* **b** could be for bed, book, banana, bus, boat, bear
* **c** could be for cat, cow, cup, cushion, cake, car
* **p** could be for pot, pig, paper, pencil, pear
* **t** could be for table, television, truck, train

Say:

We are going to play a game. We are going to try to find something in the room that starts with 'b'. [The letter is 'b' (*bee*) but say it as it sounds at the beginning of the word 'bed'.] Say the sound 'b' very softly, and encourage your child to keep saying it. Walk round the room with him slowly, saying the letter. Help him to find something – for example, a book – and go and point to it.]

What is this? This is a book. Book. Book starts with 'b'. Can you say 'b'? [Repeat the sound two or three times.] *Good. Well done!*

Now we are going to try to find something in the room that starts with 't'. [The letter is 't' (*tee*) but say it as it sounds at the beginning of the word 'table'. Say the sound 't' very softly, and encourage him to keep saying it. Walk round the room with him slowly, saying the letter. Help him to find something – for example, a table – and go and point to it.]

What is this? This is a table. Table. Table starts with 't'. Can you say 't'? Good. Well done!

Variation

Get a basket or plastic bowl. Instead of pointing to the articles when he finds them, ask your child to put them in the basket or bowl. (They will need to be small articles or toys like plastic animals.)

Once your child is very familiar with this game, let him go and find the objects himself and bring them to you:

Can you go and find me one of your animals that starts with 'd'?
Dog! Well done. Bring it back and put it in this bowl.

Note Always be guided by what your child is happy to do. As discussed in Chapter 3, there is no need to rush this game. Familiarisation may take many months, depending on when you start.

WHAT DOES IT START WITH?

Aim

To encourage your child to listen carefully for the first letter of a word (start with **Listening for letters**, page 133, and once she is familiar with that, move on to this variation). Use the Sound Chart (page 43) to pronounce the letters of the alphabet in a way that is easy to start with.

Props

An alphabet chart. You should be able to buy a chart from an educational toy shop. They are usually made of felt or cotton and have 26 pockets. On the outside of each pocket is a letter of the alphabet. Inside each pocket is an item that begins with the corresponding letter. If you have the time and inclination, you could make your own chart.

Note Many alphabet charts and books use objects that do not represent the basic sounds of the alphabet (for example, 'o' is often represented by an owl). Make up some simpler alternatives to help your child identify the basic sounds of each letter. The letter 'o', for example, would be better represented by an orange.

Play

Hang the alphabet chart on the wall or place it on the floor and sit in front of it with your child. Make the game simple to start with: take out only five items. *Can you find me something that starts with 'd'?* [The letter is 'd' (*dee*) but say it as it sounds at the beginning of the word 'dog'. Say the sound 'd' very softly, and encourage your child to keep saying it. Help her to find the item the first few times, or as long as it takes her to get the hang of the game.] *Good. Well done! Now put it back in its pocket.*

Now can you find me something that starts with 'e'? Egg – good! Now put it back in its pocket.

AGES
2½+

GUESS WHICH ANIMAL

Aim

To encourage your child to listen to and remember descriptive words – in this case, words about animals. A hiding and guessing game of any kind holds great appeal for a young child.

Props

Some small plastic animals

Play

You could play this game with your child while she is having a bath. Hide one of the animals behind your back. Your child has to guess which animal you are hiding based on the description you give her. Start simply. Say:

I am going to hide one of your little animals behind my back. I am going to tell you some things about this animal and you have to guess which animal I am hiding. Are you ready? [Take one of the animals – the duck, for example – and hide it behind your back.]

Hello, Emma. [Use your child's name, and use a funny voice as you pretend to be the duck.] *I want to have a bath. Can I come into the bath, please? I swim in the water and I say 'quack, quack'. Can you guess which animal I am?* [Help her the first few times.]

Yes, I am a duck! Well done! [Give the duck to her to put in the bath or line up on the edge. Choose another animal and use a different voice.]

Hello, Emma. I want to have a bath. Can I come into the bath, please? I wag my tail and I say 'woof, woof'. Can you guess which animal I am? Yes. I am a dog. Well done!

As she becomes familiar with more words and animal characteristics, give her clues like:

I have a very long neck and very long legs.
I have black stripes on my back and can run very fast.
I hop along and have a baby in my pouch.

More . . .

Older children will also enjoy this game but you will need to challenge them with more difficult clues.

WATER WORKS

Aim

To encourage your child to explore and discover things to do with water. You can also help her to recognise different shapes and sizes of containers. You can play this game indoors or outdoors, or in the bath (the best idea if you live in a region of water scarcity).

Props

A big plastic tub
Small plastic containers – square and round
2 plastic jugs – one small, one large

Play

Put a small amount of water in the big plastic tub (or the bath). Show your child how to pour water carefully from one container to another. As she gets the idea you will be able to let her continue by herself. Talk about the shapes and sizes of the containers as you pour:

Let's find a square container. Where is the square container? Here it is – this container is square. Let's pour some water from the small jug into the square container. [Help her.] Well done!

Now let's find a round container. Where is the round container? Here it is – this container is round. Let's pour some water into the round container. [Help her.] Well done!

Fill the big jug with water and hand it to her – you may need to help her by holding on to it. Say:

Does this big jug of water feel heavy? Yes. This big jug feels heavy. Let's pour some water from the big jug into the little jug. Where is the little jug? Here it is. Here is the little jug. [Help her to pour some water from the big jug into the little jug. Gently pour some water over her hands.] *What does the water feel like? Is it hot? No. It is not hot. Is it cold? Yes, it is cold.* Use this opportunity to talk to her a little about water and all its wonderful qualities. Use water left over to water the plants with her. Talk about how important it is to save water.

Variations

* Build an aquarium for little plastic fish, whales or sharks. Put ferns across the container so that the fish can hide under them. Use grass, leaves, seaweed, pebbles.
* Build a swimming pool for little plastic animals. Use a safe plastic tub with low edges. Ask your child if she can think of a way to make a slippery dip so that the animals can slide into the swimming pool.
* Use food colouring to colour the water.
* While playing with water, some children like to use a cloth or scrubbing brush to clean outside tables and benches, just like an adult.
* Show your child what happens when water freezes and ice melts. Use iceblock containers and experiment.

Note This game could even be used as a 'reward', as most children *love* being able to play with water. They love to feel it running through their fingers and watching it flow from one container to another.

MIMING

Aim

To give your child a chance to imitate people or animals, and in doing so, to spark his imagination and develop his memory skills. Acting comes very naturally to many young children but others will need your ideas and encouragement to help build their confidence.

Props

This game works best with a few people – it's particularly fun to play when you are on holidays or at a family gathering with lots of people around. Find an area to use as a small stage.

Play

Set up a row of chairs for the audience and have everyone sit down. If there aren't many people around, put some soft toys in the chairs instead. Be ready with ideas for your child to act out. Some ideas work better than others to start with – these include dancing, singing with a microphone, playing the piano, playing the trumpet, playing the violin, swimming, playing tennis, playing cricket, rowing a boat, driving a car, opening a gate, touching something hot, blowing out a candle, typing on the computer, pretending to be an animal (a bird flying, a snake slithering, a kangaroo hopping along with a baby in her pouch, a dog drinking milk out of a bowl, a frog jumping, a horse galloping, a crab walking sideways, a giraffe stretching, an elephant stomping, a lion roaring, a crocodile snapping).

Now, Joshua, we're going to play a miming game. You are going to pretend to do something while we watch. You don't say anything. You only act. This is called miming. What about a dog? What does a dog do? [Help him with ideas if necessary.] *Yes, he licks his food out of the bowl.*

You could pretend to be dancing. [Give him a chance to show you how he
would dance.] *You could pretend to be driving a car.* [If he needs help,
show him different ways of acting out these activities. Explain again
that this is miming only, and there is no talking. When your child feels
confident enough, he will think of ideas for himself.]

*After you have acted out the idea, we have to try to guess what you are doing.
Then, whoever gets it right has to do some miming.*

LOOKING AT LETTERS

Aim

To help your child begin to identify what a letter looks like. You can play
this game once your child is very familiar with the idea of listening for the
first sound of simple words, as in **Listening for letters** (page 133) and
What does it start with? (page 135). Touching and looking at the letter
while listening to you say it will help her to remember it.

Props

Lowercase magnetic or wooden letters of the alphabet (or, if you feel creative, your own set of lowercase alphabet cards made of material that is
interesting for your child to touch).

Note Keep using the Sound Chart (page 43) to pronounce the sounds of
the alphabet.

Play

Use the same format as **Listening for letters** but, this time, show her the letter while you say the sound of it and let her feel the shape of it. She can then hold it while she goes and identifies something in the room beginning with that letter.

Variation AGES 3½+

Think of simple words your child uses. Choose only three letters of the alphabet to begin with and put them in front of your child. Keep the others out of sight.

What letter does the word 'mum' start with? [Wait for her to respond; only prompt her if necessary.]

Good – 'm'. Now, please can you give me the letter 'm'? Well done!

What letter does the word 'dad' start with?

Good – 'd'. Now, please can you give me the letter 'd'? Well done!

 AGES 3+

DIY ALPHABET BOOK

Aim

To help your child learn the sounds and letters of the alphabet, and words that begin with each letter.

Props

A big scrapbook

Newspapers and magazines

A pen/pencil

Safe scissors

Glue

Play

Label the pages of the scrapbook with the letters (lowercase) of the alphabet – one page for each letter. Then, anytime you or your child thinks of it, cut out a picture from a magazine or newspaper and help him to stick it on the appropriate page while you talk about the letter and the picture. The scrapbook does not have to be neat; the whole idea has more impact if the child does it with you.

PLAYHOUSE

Aim

To encourage conversation as you improvise with a range of objects and materials to build a pretend house. It is the setting up of the playhouse, rather than the end result, that provides the most fun for your child. It might take a while the first time, but it becomes easier each time – and more fun, as you and your child talk about new ideas. There are endless possibilities.

Once the playhouse is built, the excitement may not last long, depending on the child's particular interests. But she may want to go back to it during the day so don't pack it up immediately.

Props

Small plastic tables or chairs

Toys

Books

Pegs

Cushions

Pillows

Old sheets and blankets or coloured pieces of material or cardboard

Decorations such as coloured pompoms

Thick string

Some old scarves (keep old scarves and pieces of brightly coloured
    material for this purpose – they are easy to store)

Play

Find a suitable area to build, either in the middle of the room under a big table, between a table and some chairs, in the area under the stairs or outside in a suitable place. Then, explain the idea to your child and follow her lead if she gives one. Every child will have a different idea of what she wants to build and what she wants to do in a playhouse. Some children want to do the washing, some want to set the table for dinner or prepare something to eat, some want to paint, some pretend to go to sleep, some pretend to go out to work in a car or on a bus. Some make up new names for themselves and their pretend pets. Some want to dress up as well.

Let's pretend we are going to make our own house now. Where will we make the front wall? Yes. We will put the front wall here. We could use this piece

of material to make the front wall of the house. What will we use to make a front door? Yes, we could make an opening here.

Tie up string and drape scarves or cover a table with a sheet if you need to make walls.

Now, where will we make the back wall? Yes. We will put the back wall here. What will we use to make a back door? Where shall we put it?

We can put some cushions on the floor for our beds. Will we put them near the wall or in the middle of the room? We can use a little table and some chairs. Where will we put this table? Where will we put the chairs?

Would you like to have a pet? What sort of pet? What will we call him? Where will he sleep?

Shall we have a garden? And what about a swimming pool for when the weather's hot? [Use green material or scarves for the garden and blue material for the pool. Make a colourful pathway from the front door to the pool with pompoms and thick string. Continue building and creating in whatever way your child suggests.

Variation

Use cushions and pillows to build a cave, a cabin, a fort, a bus or a boat.

WHAT'S MISSING?

Aim

To stimulate your child's visual sense and to develop perception and memory skills. A hiding and guessing game of any kind holds great appeal for a young child. Just play it once or twice to start with.

Props

A tray

Five small items – for example, things like a toy animal, a teaspoon, a toy car, a lemon, a hair band, a brightly coloured plastic fish, a comb, a small pencil, a little ball

A tea towel

Play

Prepare carefully before you bring your child to join you because you will lose the moment if you have to dash away to find something. Place the items on the tray then sit down with your child. First, make sure he knows the names of all the items you are using.

We are going to play a game. Let's look at the things we have got here and say their names. Here is a teaspoon. Here is a fish. Here is a lemon . . .

When you are sure he knows what everything is called, say:

Now, please turn around with your back to me, and cover your eyes with your hands. I am going to take one of these items off the tray and hide it behind my back. [When he has turned away, remove one of the items – for example, the fish – and hide it behind your back. Put the tea towel over the tray for a little extra mystery.]

Ready! You can look now. Can you tell me what is missing from the tray? [Help him if needed.] *Is it the teaspoon? No. Is it the lemon? No. Is it the fish?*

Yes. Well done! The fish is missing. I am going to put the fish over here. [Make a pile for items already used.] *Now I am going to take something else away. Please turn around.* [Hide a different item behind your back – for example, the teaspoon.]

Ready! You can look now. Can you tell me what is missing? The teaspoon – well done!

When you have done this a few times, swap roles and let your child do the hiding – if he still feels like playing.

Now it is your turn to be the teacher. You can tell me to turn around and cover my eyes while you take something off the tray. Take something away and hide it behind your back. [Turn around and put your fingers over your eyes. Give him some time to choose.]

Have you taken something away yet? Can I turn around? [It is important that you follow his instructions – he is the teacher.]

Now I have to tell you what is missing. [You can pretend to have difficulty remembering what is missing. Repeat the names of the items, as the repetition reinforces the language.]

Variation

As he becomes more skilled at observation and recall, gradually add more items to the tray.

GUESS THE SOUND

Aim

To encourage your child to concentrate on different sounds and to associate them with things in her everyday world. She will learn new words as you repeat the names of the items.

Props

Items that you have on hand and that are familiar to her – for example, two spoons, a ball, a pencil, a glass jar, a plastic jar with rice or pasta in it, a toy that makes a soft sound, a set of keys, a piece of paper

Play

Have all the items ready on the table so that your child does not have to wait. Sit beside her and discuss the items – make sure she knows what they are called. Then say:

We are going to play a guessing game. Please turn around and close your eyes. Stay very quiet. Listen carefully. I am going to use one of these things to make a noise. I want you to try to guess which thing I am using to make the noise. Here we go. [Pick up the paper and make a crunchy noise with it. Repeat the sound until she works out what it is. Help her if needed.] *I'm using the paper – well done!*

Repeat the routine with a different sound – bounce the ball on the floor, tap the pencil on the table, shake the jar with the rice/pasta, tap the glass jar with a spoon, tap two spoons together, jangle the keys, and so on. Once you have done this a few times, let her be the teacher.

Variations

Include things that you can do yourself – clap your hands, whistle, tap your fingers on the table.

Listen for noises around the house – washing machine, mobile phone, clock. Listen for noises from outside – car, plane, dog, lawn mower, a bird call, the wind in the trees, the rain falling, the sound of a drill. Take her to where the sound is coming from and compare it with something else she has heard.

WHERE AM I?

Aim

To motivate your child to listen carefully to your voice as he learns how to hide.

Props

Good places in your home for hiding!

Play

Choose possible hiding places with your child – not too far from the 'starting post' where you are going to close your eyes while he hides. He could hide behind a door, a chair or the sofa, or under a table. You (as the finder) have to walk to different areas nearby, pretending to look everywhere for him.

At first, you will need to help him to hide (or get someone else to help him). Explain that he has to stay there until you find him. Depending on his age, this may take many attempts. Explain that when he hides, he will have to stay very quiet, otherwise you will hear him and know where he is. As he becomes more familiar with the game, get his ideas on where he could hide. (Make sure they are safe.) Tell him you will call out, 'Coming to find you!' and he has to listen. As you walk around, talk out loud and keep repeating words so that he learns new words each time you play. Make sure that your child can hear you. Use lots of expression in your voice and vary it each time as you pose a question, make a statement, or express disappointment when you cannot find him. For example:

Coming to find you! Knock, knock. Is Henry behind the kitchen door? [Check behind the kitchen door.] *No, I can't see him there. Henry is not behind the kitchen door. I wonder where he is. I'll try the chair . . . Is Henry behind the chair?* [Check behind the chair.] *No, I can't see him there. He is not behind the chair. I wonder where he is. I'll try under the kitchen table . . . Knock, knock. Is Henry under the kitchen table?* [Check under the kitchen table.] *No, I can't see him there. I wonder where he is. I'll have to look in the cupboard . . .* [After a while, go to wherever he is hiding and discover him. One of my dearest little friends, at age three, would always jump out when I came near and roar like a lion to scare me!]

Variation

Bring numbers into the game. Count to ten out loud so your child can hear, then call out, 'Coming ready or not!' as you start the game.

WHAT DOES THIS FEEL LIKE?

Aim

To help your child listen to and remember descriptive words, and recognise objects by feeling their shape and/or texture.

Props

Six small objects with interesting shapes and/or textures – for example,
   a toy car, a velvet or silk scarf, a hairbrush, a sponge, a small soft toy,
   a wooden toy, a spoon, a plastic cup, a piece of sandpaper, a small
   pebble or stone, a shell, a leaf, a plastic ring, a soft rubber ball, a
   straw, some elastic, a pine cone
A big cloth bag or pillow case in which you can put the items

Play

Put the six items on the table and have the bag ready beside you. Sit down with your child and talk briefly about each item.

We are going to play a game with these things. [Hand her one of the
   things – for example, the wooden toy.] *This wooden toy is hard. Feel this
   toy. This toy is hard.* [Take the wooden toy, put it in the bag and hand her
   the soft toy.] *This teddy bear is soft, fluffy and furry.*

Continue in the same way (the hairbrush is prickly, the rubber ball is squishy, the elastic is stretchy, the scarf is velvety and smooth, and so on) until you've put all the items into the bag. Then say:

*Please turn your head away and close your eyes – don't peek. Now, put your
   hand inside the bag* [guide her hand] *and feel one thing. Have you found
   something? Keep it in your hand, inside the bag, and tell me what it feels
   like without looking at it. Don't peek – just feel it with your hand.* [Help her
   with ideas to describe it if she does not know.] *What does it feel like? Is*

it hard? Is it soft? You think it feels hard? Bring it out. Yes – well done! It is
hard. It is the wooden toy. Put it on the table. Thank you.
Now turn your head away and close your eyes again. Put your hand inside the
bag. Feel one thing, keep your hand inside the bag and tell me what it feels
like. Don't peek. Just feel it. [Help her again . . .]

Continue like this for one more item and then ask her if she would like to
be the teacher. Follow her instructions and continue playing the game.

Variations

Have three hard and three soft toys in the bag. When you have pulled
them all out of the bag, sort them into soft and hard categories.

Gently draw with your finger on the palm of your child's hand. Draw, for
example, a squiggly line, a circle, some straight lines, some dots, and
ask her what it feels like.

FLOAT OR SINK?

Aim

To help your child investigate different materials – plastic, paper, wood,
stone – and use descriptive words.

Props

The kitchen sink, or a large plastic tub, with some water in it

A collection of items such as a bottle cap, a piece of recycled paper, a big stone, a little pebble, flower petals, leaves, bark, a pencil, a cork and an empty plastic bottle

Play

Put each item in the water, one at a time. For example, tear up small pieces of paper and say:

Let's put a piece of paper into the water and see what happens. [Put a piece of paper into the water.] *Look – this piece of paper floats on top of the water. It is very light.* [Let your child put a few pieces of paper in the water and watch them floating.]

Let's put this stone into the water and see what happens. [Drop the stone into the tub.] *Look – this stone drops to the bottom very quickly. It sinks. It is heavy.* [Let your child put a stone into the water.]

Let's put this bottle cap into the water and see what happens. [Drop the bottle cap into the water.] *Look – the bottle cap floats on top of the water. It is light. It is made of plastic.*

AGES
3+

LET'S INVESTIGATE

Aim

To encourage your child's curiosity and expand her vocabulary by talking about some familiar household items. Take the time to tell her what they are, what they are made of and a little bit about what happens when you use them.

Props

Whatever you have in the rooms of your house – doors, windows, taps, furniture, appliances, mirrors, handles, lights

Play

Focus on one or two household items when the opportunity presents itself. Hold your child's hand and walk over to the item together. For example, in the kitchen, you could go to the fridge and say:

This is our fridge. [Open the door of the fridge.] *Why do we put food in the fridge? We put food in the fridge to keep it cool so that it is safe to eat. We must SHUT the fridge door to keep things cool.* [Show her the freezer compartment.] *It is VERY cold in the freezer – look at the ice. We put food in the freezer so that it will keep safely for a long time. We put ice-cream in the freezer so that it won't melt. We put water in these little containers so that they will freeze and become iceblocks.*

Or, when you're in the bathroom, you could say:

This is the bathroom. This is a tap. It is made of metal. When we turn this handle, some water comes out of the tap – sometimes it is hot, sometimes it is cold. [Show her.] *You must always check to see whether the water is too hot before you wash your hands. You must always check the water before you get in the bath to see whether it is too hot or too cold.*

How does the water get into the tap? Where does the water go when we pull out the plug?

Another time, you could focus on the lights. Say:

How many lights are there in this room? We turn the lights on at night-time when it is dark outside. We turn them off when we don't need to use them.

Let's turn off all the lights now and see how dark it is. [You could then turn on a torch or light some candles.]

Can you find a dark place in the house to hide?

You could concentrate on safety issues in different rooms of the house – but just when you happen to be in each room, not all at once!

If you jump near the edge of the bed, you might fall off and hurt your head.

If you touch this, you might burn yourself.

If you only turn the tap on a little way when you are washing your hands, the water won't splash you.

If you drop anything made of glass, it will smash into pieces.

If there is water on the floor, you might slip.

AGES
4+

PIANO TIME

For those who play the piano, even a little.

Aim

To familiarise your child with the piano, make her familiar with its uses and possibilities and, above all, show her why you love the piano and the sound it makes.

Props

A piano or keyboard

Play

Sit down with your child at the piano and try ONE of the following ideas, just for two minutes to begin with.

Talk about the black and white notes:

* touch some black notes
* touch some white notes
* show her some octaves and use the word
* show her all the Cs
* show her all the Gs
* show her all the E flats

Let her 'play' the piano and make up names for the kind of music she is playing. For example:

* if she plays gently, it could be rain music or tiptoe-walking music
* if she plays heavily, it could be dinosaur music
* if she plays rhythmically, like walking, it could be duck or penguin music
* if she plays fast music with lots of notes, it could be busy-ant music
* if she pretends to climb over the notes with her fingers, it could be crab music

Play a tune:

Put her hand on the keys and get her to close her fingers into a little ball. Then tell her to slowly 'wake up' each finger, stretch it out but keep it curved, until all five fingers are ready to play the notes. Show her how to play 'Hot cross buns', for example. Play the first two bars only, then get your child to imitate you. That is enough for the first day.

Another day, play the next two bars.

Another day, put these four bars together.

When she can confidently play the whole tune, you can put chords in the bass and play with her.

Play duets:

Show her how to play two or three notes in the treble and you work out a bass to accompany her.

SIMON SAYS

Aim

To encourage your child to concentrate and follow instructions as you call out things for him to do.

Props

The game works better with several players but you can still make it fun with just you and your child.

Play

We are going to play a game. You have to concentrate very hard! I am going to pretend that I am called Simon. I am going to call out things for you to do. You must do ONLY what Simon says. He will tell you what to do. If he does not say 'Simon says', you must not do it! [Go through the routine with your child first to make sure he gets the idea.]

Simon says, 'Touch your head!' [Do the actions with your child.]

Simon says, 'Touch your foot!'

Simon says, 'Touch your nose!'

Simon says, 'Touch your leg!'

Simon says, 'Run to the door!'

Simon says, 'Jump three times!'

Simon says, 'Hop on one foot!'

Touch your arm! [Suddenly say this without saying 'Simon says'.] Your child must not touch his arm because Simon did not tell him to do it. If he has touched his arm, he is OUT and he becomes the next Simon and calls out the instructions to the other players/you.

FIND THE 'C' IN 'CAT'

Aim

To interest your child in recognising the look and sound of letters and, eventually, small words. You can begin playing this hide-and-seek game once your child is very familiar with listening for the sound and then recognising the look of letters (by playing games such as **Listening for letters** (page 133), **What does it start with?** (page 135), **Looking at letters** (page 141) and other playgroup or preschool activities.

Props

Paper or cardboard on which to write words. Cut out cards of appropriate size. Write simple and familiar words on one side of each card using lowercase letters. Start with three-letter words only – *cat, pen, dog, hat, man*. Keep the cards for future use.

Play

Start with five cards. Say:

Now close your eyes while I hide these five cards. [Place them around the room at your child's level so that she can enjoy walking around the room looking for them. There is no need for the cards to be completely hidden.]

These cards have words written on them. I want you to look for the first letter of the word. Can you please find me a card that starts with 'c' – 'c' for 'cat'? [Say the letter as you have pronounced it in earlier games. As she goes around the room looking for the card starting with 'c', you might need to stay near her to provide clues – you don't want her to give up looking.]

Good – 'c' for cat. Well done!

Now can you please find me a card that starts with 'p' – 'p' for 'pen'? [Help her again until she finds it.] *Good work!*

Can you please find me a card that starts with 'd'?
'd' for 'dog'?
Good work. Well done!

Variation

AGES 4½+

When your child becomes more familiar with the cards (this will be a very gradual process), ask her to look for the whole word rather than just the first letter. You can also start to introduce some longer words that she might have started to recognise by sight through other forms of play or discussion or through reading books (for example, 'dinosaur', 'farm', 'banana', 'milk', 'grass').

Can you please find me the card that says 'kite'? Good. Well done!
Can you please find me the card that says 'ball'? Good. Well done!

📖 (abc) **AGES 4+**

TREASURE HUNT

Aim

To encourage your child to read and understand simple instructions. Finding some treasure is a great motivator! If you play this regularly with your child, he will gradually begin to recognise some of the words.

Props

❋ Three little 'surprises' wrapped up in tinfoil, crepe or cellophane paper – for example, small toys your child hasn't seen for a while, little plastic animals or a little treat to eat. Use only three per game to start with. Hide the parcels in safe and easy places around the house.

✻ Paper or cardboard on which to write clues. Prepare three written clues on separate cards, describing where the surprises are hidden. Write in lowercase letters, use familiar words and simple instructions.

Play

This game is called a treasure hunt. I have hidden something special for you somewhere in the house. These words will give us a clue about where it is hidden.

Read the first clue slowly with him, pointing to each word as you read, and discuss what the clue might mean.

What does it say on this piece of paper? It says, 'Look under your pillow.' [Let him go to his bed – go with him if he wants you to. When he finds the surprise, let him unwrap it.] *What did you find? What's in there? Well done!*

Now read the second clue:

What does it say on this piece of paper? It says, 'Look under your chair.' What did you find? What's in there? Well done!'

Variation

To extend the hide-and-seek element of this game, you could hide the clues as well and have him find three or four clues first, before he finds the surprise.

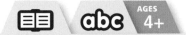

NO DOGS ALLOWED!

Aim

To focus your child's attention on print as a natural part of her day.

Play

* Point out signs, labels, recipes and other simple lists of instructions to your child as you go about daily activities with her.

* Read road signs to her, and discuss what they mean. (Sometimes these signs are only pictures or symbols without words, but it is important for her to glean the meaning from pictures as well.) For example:

  That sign says 'Stop'!

  That sign says 'Tunnel'.

  That sign says 'Look left'.

  That sign says 'No swimming'.

  That sign say 'No dogs allowed'.

* Read labels on groceries when you are out shopping with her.

* Stick some simple signs and labels on things or boxes of toys that she uses – 'cars', 'pens', 'puzzles', 'books' 'dinosaurs'.

* By age four you can start pointing to the words occasionally as you read books together. You don't need to use your finger under every word as you read; just point out one or two words every so often (see Chapter 2).

* Try putting a whiteboard in a place where you spend a lot of time – perhaps near your eating area. Start writing things on it – the date, lists of things you need to buy or little pieces of family 'news', like 'Sophie had eggs for breakfast'. Gradually, she will come up with her own ideas and ask you to write them on the board. She may even imitate you by trying to write them herself.

SCHOOLS

Aim

To give your child an opportunity to express himself by speaking in a pretend classroom and taking on the role of teacher. Children usually love this game and there are endless variations.

Props

A suitable desk and chair for the teacher
'Desks' or cushions for the pupils
A whiteboard and marker or a blackboard and chalk
Some books and scrap paper, pencils, stickers/stars
Soft toys

Play

Prepare the classroom with your child. Set up the desk and chair and the whiteboard and marker for the teacher. Arrange stickers, a pencil and a book on the teacher's desk. Set up a desk for your child and cushions for the soft toys – they will be the pupils. You be the teacher first:

Let's pretend we are at school. I am the teacher. My name is Mr Fish. [Sit down at your desk.] *Good morning, everyone.* [Hand out some pencils and paper, and discuss what you would like the pupils to draw. Walk around the classroom. Say 'Good work! Good work!' and hand out some stickers/stars.]

It is time for a story now. Please put away your pencils and paper. I will read you a story and show you the pictures. [Read a short story.]

Variations

Pretend that one of the children is being naughty. For example, if he is talking while you read, explain that this spoils the story for the other children.

Or if he won't share the pencils, discuss why it is kind to share. You could explain that the teacher might feel annoyed when children are naughty. Swap roles, letting your child be the teacher.

AGES
4+

I'M A DOCTOR

Aim

To help your child to put herself in someone else's shoes, and to learn and say new words from a specific setting – this time, the doctor's surgery.

Props

A doctor's bag, including a pretend thermometer and stethoscope (you can easily make those)

A plastic syringe

Some bandaids and a bandage

When your child is older, she can have a pen and notebook and pretend to write prescriptions and bills

Play

Your child can be the doctor. Ask her to make up a name for herself, and teach her the polite way to greet a new patient. You are the patient so lie down on the bed or floor. If your leg is sore, for example, your child can investigate.

Doctor: *Good morning, Mr Bluego. How can I help you this morning? I see you can't walk very well. What is the matter?*

Mr Bluego: *I hurt my leg. My leg is sore.*

Doctor: *What did you do to it?*

Mr Bluego: *I fell down some stairs in the garden.*

Doctor: (gently) *I am sorry to hear that. There is no need to be afraid. First, I'll have to test your leg and see if it is broken. Can you bend your knee, please? Thank you. Your leg is not broken – that is good. But I see you have a cut, so I will put some cream on your leg to make it better, and then I will put a bandage on it.*

Variations

Swap roles; you can be the doctor.

Be a vet and pretend that one of the soft toys has been hurt. Pat the toy gently, speak softly and kindly, and say things like: *Don't be frightened, little bird. We will look after you.*

AGES
4+

DOMINOES

Aim

To encourage your child to recognise that the arrangements of dots on dominoes form a pattern, and that some of the patterns are the same and match up with one another.

Props

A set of dominoes. This game is for dominoes with dots; if you have dominoes with pictures, change the language to suit the pictures.

Play

Lay the dominoes face up on the table or floor. Your child can help you divide the dominoes equally between the players. Explain that each domino has two halves with dots at either end. You can help him start the game by putting one of his dominoes in the middle of the table:

You choose one of your dominoes and put it in the middle of the table. Good. [Let's say he has chosen a domino with four dots at one end and two at the other end.]

Now I have to see if I can match the four dots or the two dots with one of my dominoes. If it matches, it looks the same. Yes – look. I have a domino with four dots. It looks the same, it matches with yours. [Put the two fours together.] *My domino only has one dot at the other end. Now, it is your turn.* [He can try to match up at the end of either domino, so he will need a one or a two. Help him at first.] *Do you have a domino with one dot or two dots?* [Help him to match it at the correct end.]

Repeat this until you cannot match up with either of the dominoes on the table.

You (or I) can't go this time. If we can't go, we knock on the floor and miss a turn.

The winner of the game is the first player to get rid of all their dominoes.

Variation

Demonstrate the domino effect! Line up all the dominoes in a row, standing them on end with only a small distance in between. If you do it correctly, you can flick your finger, tipping the first domino and causing all the others to fall down in succession.

SNAP!

Aim

To help your child to concentrate and to recognise patterns. Like dominoes, Snap! will help her to understand that some patterns are the same as others – that they match and make a pair.

Props

A pack of cards with numbers – or, if you have cards with pictures instead, change the language to suit the pictures.

Play

Sit at a table or on the floor with your child and deal out half the pack to each player. If you think it is too hard to play with the whole pack at first, sort the pack and use only the numbers from two to six, for example. Leave your child's cards on the table face down as her hand is probably still too small to hold them all. Explain *her* pile and *your* pile of cards, and show her a few examples of pairs.

Now, we're going to put one card from your pile on to the table with the numbers facing up, like this. [Show her how to pick a card from her pile and put it face up in the middle of the table.]

Then I will put my card on top of yours – like this, in the middle of the table. [Put your card on top of hers.] *If you see two cards the same on the table, one after the other, you put your hand on top of them and say 'SNAP!'*

Now you put another card from your pile on to the table. [See if she can do it by herself. If not, help her again.] *Well done.*

Keep doing this until there is a pair.

Look! A pair. These two cards are the same. Can you see these two cards? What are they? They are both fours. When this happens, we put our hand on top of those cards and say 'SNAP!' [Explain each time it happens that pairs look the same.]

Playing a game like this makes it easy to learn about pairs but it will take a little while for your child to get the idea; at first, she may want to do everything else except put the cards one on top of the other.

123 AGES 4+

WHAT'S THE TIME, MR WOLF?

Aim

To enjoy some physical activity while learning to concentrate and listen carefully for numbers.

Props

A flat area – indoors or outdoors – with enough room for taking steps and running back to 'home base'.

Play

You will take the part of Mr Wolf to start the game. Explain that you will stand at one end of the room facing the wall, while your child stands at the other end of the room. She has to ask Mr Wolf what time it is. If he says 'Two o'clock', then she counts out loud as she takes two steps towards him. If he says 'Four o'clock', then she takes four steps. And if he says 'Dinner time', then she has to run back to home base (the place where she started) before he catches her.

What's the time, Mr Wolf? [Ask your child to call this out. Mr Wolf answers by saying any time between one and twelve o'clock.]

Four o'clock. [Help your child at first to count out four steps as she walks towards you. Encourage her to say the numbers out loud – this way she 'feels' each step as she says the number. Then you face the wall again and ask your child to call out to Mr Wolf again.]

What's the time, Mr Wolf?

Two o'clock! [Help your child to count out two more steps as she walks towards you.]

Continue like this until she gets quite close, then surprise her by saying:

Dinner time! [Turn and run after her, pretending to catch her before she reaches home base. Then it is her turn to be Mr Wolf.]

Variation

Your child could take steps towards Mr Wolf by hopping or jumping instead of walking.

SHOPS

Aim

To give your child practice with sorting and matching (as she arranges the shop), and numbers and money (as she counts out change). Like other role play games, this game also provides an opportunity to learn and say new words, and to be polite and helpful.

Props

Low tables or boxes

Plastic containers

Card or paper for price signs

Money (use plastic counters if you have any or make pretend money out of
   paper notes – $1, $2, $3, $4 and $5)

A toy cash register, if you have one; if you don't, you could make a simple
   one out of a box or, of course, just pretend

Items for sale, depending on the type of shop

Play

Discuss with your child what sort of shop she wants – a toy shop, a book
shop, a garden shop, a jewellery shop, a cushion shop, a fruit and vegetables shop, or whatever she suggests. (Some children have very definite
ideas about what they want to sell!) In this example, we'll use a toy shop.
Then, together with your child, prepare the shop for the first customer.
Enjoy setting out the items for sale so that they will attract customers.
Sort the toys into crayons, cars, books, planes, blocks (which can be
further sorted into colours or shapes), coloured fish and so on. Say the
crayons cost $1, the cars cost $2 and the books cost $3. Let her watch as
you write out the price signs on pieces of paper. Count out the money with
her and put it in piles or in the cash register. She is going to be the shopkeeper and you are going to be the customer.

Pretend to be a customer coming in through a door and say:

Good morning. [Encourage your child to put on a polite 'shopkeeper' voice,
   encourage her to greet you and ask if she can help you.]

Good morning. Can I help you?

*Yes, please. I would like to buy a book for my little daughter, Anna, who is at
   home in bed. She has a bad cough.* [Your child can show you the books

in the shop. Encourage her to be helpful and talk about the books she is showing you.]

We have lots of different books. What kind of book would your daughter like?

I think she would like a book about dogs. She just loves dogs. Do you have any books about dogs? [She will probably say yes. If she says yes, ask her what happens in the book. If she says no, but suggests something else, go along with it. It can be very entertaining when she has her own ideas.]

This book looks very good. [Flip through the pages.] *That is a good idea, thank you very much. How much does the book cost?*

It costs $3, please.

Well that is fine, thank you. Here is $3. Thank you for your help. Goodbye!

Variations

The variations on the 'shop' theme are endless. For example, you could collect the best of your child's paintings and save them for an art gallery SALE! Talk about the price and write the price on the back of each painting. You could set up a cafe beside the shop and sell coffee, water and cupcakes as well.

123 | AGES 4+

MEMORY

Aim

To encourage your child to recognise shapes and patterns and to learn about pairs. This game will help to develop his memory as he tries to remember the position of the different cards on the table.

Props

A pack of cards. They don't have to be number cards – any pack of cards that can be sorted into pairs will work, but we use an ordinary pack of number cards in this example.

Play

To start with, use only five pairs of cards from the pack (numbers two to six). Put the rest of the pack aside. Sit on the floor with your child, shuffle the cards and spread them face down. Show your child how to turn over one card and then turn it back over again in exactly the same spot, face down, so that the number cannot be seen. It is sometimes difficult for a young child to pick up new cards from a shiny surface, so play on a rug.

We are going to play a game of Memory. We will look for two cards that are the same. First we turn over one card like this [turn over a card and leave it face up in exactly the same place].

This is a five [show him the card]. *I leave the card like this so that you can see it, and I say the number out loud.* [Saying the number out loud reinforces the learning.]

Now, I am going to try to find another five, to match this one. I am looking for a five . . . I am looking for a five . . . [Turn over another card.]

Well – is this a five? No – what is it? It is a six. It is not the same as the first card, is it? So we turn both cards back, face down, in exactly the same spot so that we can remember where they are for next time. [Turn both cards back face down. Encourage your child to try to remember what they are, even though he can't see them.]

Now it is your turn. Turn over a card – any card you like. What is it? [Help him if he needs help.] *This is a four. Now turn over another card. What is it? It is a three. It is not the same as the first card, is it? No. So we turn both cards back over again.*

My turn again. Look – a five! I think there was another five somewhere over here . . . yes! I've got two fives. We call them a pair. When you get a pair, you keep the pair in a little pile beside you. That is your pile of cards. The winner is the person who gets the most pairs.

Continue playing until there are no cards left face down, then help your child to count how many pairs you both have.

Variation

When he begins to understand the game, gradually add the numbers seven and eight, then nine and ten, and finally the jacks, queens, kings and aces.

GUESS WHAT I'M CLAPPING

Aim

To motivate your child to concentrate and listen carefully to a rhythm.

Play

Choose a familiar song or nursery rhyme but don't tell your child what it is. Say:

This is a song you know but I am only going to clap the rhythm. Listen carefully and see whether you can work out what song this is. [Clap out the rhythm of the song/rhyme you have chosen.]

Can you tell me what tune I was clapping? [Help him until he gets the idea. You can play this game while you are walking along or waiting for someone or something, or while your child is in the bath. Before you know it, he will be wanting to clap one for you.]

JUMP THE WORD

Aim

To help your child to recognise the 'look' of some familiar words (like **Find the 'c' in 'cat'**, page 158). The physical element adds great enjoyment.

Props

Paper or cardboard on which to write words. Cut out cards of appropriate size. Write simple and familiar words on one side of each card using lowercase letters. Start with three-letter words only, for example:

rat, bug, cow, sun, fox

mum, bus, dog, pig, dad

bat, hat, mat, cat, rat

red, bed, zip, lip, dip

dig, jug, mug, sun, bun

Keep the cards for future use.

Play

Choose five cards and place them on the floor like the rungs of a ladder, with plenty of space between each card. Hold your child's hand, and go and look at each word on the floor. Say the word on the first card and jump over it together. Say the word on the second card and jump over it together. Continue like this. Then say:

Look carefully. I am going to ask you to jump over a card on the floor. Can you please find the card that says 'rat'? Jump over the card that says 'rat'. Jump over the card and bring it to me, please.' [Help him with the words he doesn't know.] *Thank you. Well done. I am going to keep the cards in a pile beside me.*

Look carefully. I am going to ask you to jump over another card. Can you please find the card that says 'bug'? Jump over the card that says 'bug' and bring it to me, please. [Help him again. You will know when your child is ready to do it by himself.]

Look carefully. I am going to ask you to jump over another card on the floor. Can you please find the card that says 'cow'. Jump over the card that says 'cow' and bring it to me, please.

Follow the same pattern for the rest of the five words you have chosen, then stop. This is enough for the first time. Next time, play with the same words. The time after, play with new words.

Variation

Swap roles: your child becomes the teacher and asks you to jump over the words you have chosen together.

Appendix 1

ACTIVITIES AND IDEAS FOR BABIES (0–12 MONTHS)

THE NEW BABY – AN OVERWHELMING TIME FOR PARENTS

A BABY'S FIRST YEAR is an extraordinary time for parents. If this is your first child, it's a life-altering experience. If this is your second, third or fourth child, life just becomes increasingly chaotic. The tasks of feeding, changing nappies and trying to console a new baby can be completely overwhelming, leaving you with little time to do much else.

You will want to read about the milestones for your baby's physical development and there are many websites and books to help you there. Our aim here is very simple: to provide you with a selection of play activities to help you through the first year. When you are tired, it's very easy to forget the progress you are making in forging a new relationship. These activities are designed to help you start to communicate with this tiny human bundle and enjoy some precious moments in your child's first year.

WHILE HE'S LISTENING TO YOU . . .

✳ Talk to your baby while you are changing his nappy and as you walk around with him. There is no need for 'baby talk' – just playful chatter about the things that are going on around him.

✳ Sing him lullabies while you rock him in your arms or gently on your knees before bedtime. For example (see Appendix 3 for lyrics):
  × 'Hush-a-bye-baby'
  × 'Lula lula bye bye'
  × 'Twinkle, twinkle, little star'

✳ Sing at other times as well. Choose any of your favourite songs, but you will find that some songs appeal to your baby more than others. Nursery rhymes that use alliteration and repeat rhyming words are usually the most popular; your baby will love the sound of these words, even if you don't. Some easy songs to start with include:
  × 'Baa baa black sheep'
  × 'Do you know the muffin man?'
  × 'Doe, a deer'
  × 'Five little ducks'
  × 'Frère Jacques'
  × 'London Bridge is falling down'
  × 'Row, row, row your boat'

✳ Hold your baby's hands and gently move them with yours while you sing or talk to him. Or, move his legs very gently as if he were on a bicycle.

✳ Say rhymes as you play with his hands and fingers. For example (see Appendix 3 for lyrics):
  × 'This little pig went to market'
  × 'Round and round the garden'
  × 'Two little dicky birds sitting on a wall'

- × 'Incy Wincy spider'
- × 'Where is Thumbkin?'
- ✱ When your baby starts to make *er er er* and *ah ah ah* sounds, keep repeating these sounds back to him.

WHILE HE'S WATCHING YOU . . .

- ✱ Vary your facial expressions (smile, surprise, frown) and exaggerate the movement of your mouth as you are talking and singing to him.
- ✱ Put your baby where he can see you while you are working.
- ✱ Lie him on a rug on the floor and string up things for him to look at – for example, a black-and-white mobile with geometric patterns or a baby gym.
- ✱ Prop up some cards on a cushion on the change-table beside him or hold one up near your face and move it around a little. (You can buy or make cards about the size of your hand with bold black-and-white geometric patterns on them – two or three large black dots, a target ring, a triangle, four squares, or a noughts-and-crosses grid.)
- ✱ Show him brightly coloured toys.
- ✱ Show him some brightly coloured wrapping paper or shiny, crinkly paper such as tinfoil.
- ✱ Show him things while he is having a bath – your hands, his hands, his feet, a plastic duck, or water pouring out of a jug. Talk about these things – you don't need to say much.
- ✱ Let him watch your fingers . . .
  - × Click your fingers together as you circle your arm about, or just bring your thumb and forefinger together (like a bird's beak) as you move your arm slowly from side to side and up and down.

- × 'Walk' your fingers from his level up as high as you can go, saying 'up, up, up' and making your voice go higher and higher. Then bring your fingers and voice down as you say 'down, down, down'.

AS HE BECOMES MORE RESPONSIVE . . .

* Start playing the earliest form of hide-and-seek with your baby – put your fingers over your face and pull them away again as you say 'boo!'
* Play with a torch – shine the light up on the ceiling or on the wall.
* Blow bubbles up into the air with a bubble blower.
* Sit down with him and roll a ball along the floor to him.
* Show him a ball then cover it with a cloth. Take off the cloth.
* Hide a toy and ask him: *Where's the penguin gone?* Keep asking *Where's the penguin?* as you pretend to look everywhere but the right place. Finally, discover the penguin!
* Wrap something up (a soft toy, for example – it doesn't need to be new; one that he already knows is fine) in soft paper, perhaps two or three layers, then give it to him to unwrap.
* Encourage him to imitate you by doing and saying things like:
  - × *hands on **head**, hands on head*
  - × *hands on **nose**, hands on nose*
  - × *hands in the **air**, hands in the air*
* Vary the tone and pitch of your voice as you talk to your baby. Talk to him, then whisper the same sentence or word. **Use a** high voice then a low voice.
* Repeat one sound or word at a time. Some words are much easier for your baby to imitate because of the way they sound or look to him – exaggerate the movement of your lips. Try words with these sorts of sounds:

- *mum mum mum*
- *dad dad dad*
- *bub bub bub – bubba – bye bye*
- *wow!*
- *wash, fish, ssshhh* [extend the *sh* sound]
- *la la la la la* [try singing this into a mirror – you can see why your baby loves this sound as he watches you]
- *up, up, up* [as you lift him out of the cot or out of the stroller]
- *hello hello*
- *well well well*
- *dear dear dear*

✻ Imitate an animal or bird sound. For example:
- What does the dog say? *woof woof*
- What does the cat say? *miaow*
- What does the cow say? *mooo*
- What does the kookaburra say? *uw uw uw ah ah ah*
- What does the pig say? *oink oink*
- What does the horse say? *wheeeee*
- What does the bee say? *bzzzzz*
- What does the rooster say? *cock-a-doodle-doo*

✻ Make funny faces and sounds. You will soon work out which particular things make him laugh. For example, you could:
- pretend to cough
- pretend to sneeze
- pretend to laugh – say *ha ha ha* in some form or other
- make clicking noises with your tongue on the roof of your mouth
- make your lips buzz
- imitate the *tick, tock, tick, tock* of a clock
- imitate the whistle of a train, the *vroom vroom* noise of a car, the *putt putt* of a boat or the *chop chop* sound of a helicopter

* put on a funny voice for one of his toys
* make bird noises
* talk to him through a cardboard roll
* rub your fingers over your lips and make a sound at the same time
* squeeze toys that make a noise when squeezed

❉ Make up little rhymes, using your child's name:
Dance and sing, dance and sing
Vadim loves to dance and sing
or:
Clap hands, Etta
Clap hands, Etta
or:
Toby is a very good boy
He's a good little boy – wheeeee! [hoist him up in the air]

❉ Talk to him while you are doing things with him. If you say the same word every time you do a certain action, he will learn to expect you to say those words. One day, he will find them easy to imitate because he has heard them so often:
Sit down with Dad. Here's your book. Open the book.
One, two, three – and into the bath!
Shut the door. Off we go. Wave goodbye.

❉ Tell him the name of familiar things he touches:
This is your bear. Bear.
This is your chair. Chair.

❉ Tell him the names of things he sees as you look out the window or take him for a walk in the stroller:
There's a car. There's a plane. There's a red flower.
See the dog? See the leaves on the trees? See the clouds in the sky?

❉ When he is sitting in front of you, or in the bath, say:

That's your head. Head.

That's your nose. Nose.

❋ Continue to sing nursery rhymes and songs, especially ones with funny words and repetition. For example, sing 'Five little ducks' (see page 188) while he is having a bath – use your fingers to act as the five little ducks and have a rubber duck for Mother Duck. He won't mind if you sing that same song every night *and* do exactly the same actions – in fact, he will look forward to it.

❋ Have CDs ready to play in the kitchen, the car, or your child's bedroom (play soothing music before bedtime).

❋ Encourage him to shake maracas or rattles, especially when you have music playing.

❋ Let him touch things of different textures, for example:
 × soft – like muslin
 × soft and silky – like a furry toy animal
 × hard – like a small toy telephone
 × smooth – like velvet
 × rough – like sandpaper
 × scratchy – like a little straw basket
 × spongy – like a sponge
 × curved – like a plastic toy
 × round – like a small ball
 × cold – like a spoon

❋ Encourage his fine-motor skills with the activities listed on page 67 (Hands-on).

BOOKS AND BABIES

It is never too early to start reading to your child. For some ideas, see Chapter 2.

Appendix 2
FARAWAY GRANDPARENTS

IF YOU HAVE GRANDCHILDREN who live a long distance away and you can't play games with them, you have to make the most of your time on the phone (or Skype, if you have it). Work out what to talk about and try asking questions that will encourage her thoughts and words, and lead on to further discussion. This often works better than questions that can just be answered with a 'Yes' or a 'No'. For example:

* *What is your cat/dog doing?*
* *What are you building?*
* *Where did you go today? How did you get there?*
* *What did you see at the park?*
* *How did you help Mum today?*

When she has finished all she has to tell, give her a surprise by asking her a question like one of these, for a change:

* *What are our eyes for?*
* *What makes you laugh/cry/gives you a fright?*

*   *Where does the water go when you pull out the plug?*
*   *How wide can you stretch your arms?*
*   *Where do your cousins live? Where does your uncle live?*
*   *Would you like to sing me a song?*

If you ask questions often enough, you will find that young children soon have questions to ask you. Be prepared for questions such as: *What have you been doing today? Will you make a cactus garden for me? Will you get a fish tank for me?*

STORYTELLING AND DISCUSSION

Most young children love to listen to you telling them a story (see Chapter 2). It doesn't have to be long; they'll be fascinated by an incident involving a person or an animal that they know. Some ideas for storytelling over the phone include:

*   an anecdote about something that happened to you that day – incorporate any of the child's special interests into the story
*   something you saw today – perhaps a snail or a lizard – and where you found it. Spark her curiosity!
*   a story about her when she was a baby
*   a story about her parents when they were little
*   a story about you when you were her age – where you lived, what you played.

Many children are fascinated by imagining what their grandparents did when they were children.

LOOKING AROUND

If your grandchild is carrying a cordless phone, you can say:

Can you go to your bedroom and tell me what it looks like today?

Let her describe as much as possible without you prompting her, and then ask her questions. When she is old enough, you can turn this discussion into a 'words and letters' game (as in **Listening for letters** on page 133) by asking questions like:

✳ *Can you see anything in your room beginning with 'w'?* [window, wall]

✳ *'d'?* [door, desk]

✳ *'t'?* [table, toys]

HIDING AND GUESSING

Even on the phone, you'll be amazed by how much amusement young children can get from a hiding-and-guessing game. For example, you could say to your grandchild:

Would you like to go and find your favourite toy? Then hide it somewhere in your room. Don't tell me where you have hidden it – I will try to guess where it is and I will keep guessing until I say the right place. You can give me a little clue if you like.

Appendix 3
SONG LYRICS/NURSERY RHYMES

LULLABIES

Hush-a-bye-baby, on the tree top,
When the wind blows the cradle will rock;
When the bow breaks, the cradle will fall,
And down will come baby, cradle and all.

Singing lula lula lula lula bye-bye
Do you want the moon to play with?
Or the stars to run away with?
They are yours if you do not cry . . .

      *   *   *

Singing lula lula lula lula bye-bye
In your mammy's arms come creeping
And soon you'll be a-sleeping
Singing lula lula lula lula bye . . .

Twinkle, twinkle, little star,
How I wonder what you are!

Up above the world so high,
Like a diamond in the sky,
Twinkle, twinkle, little star,
How I wonder what you are!

ACTION SONGS

This little pig went to market [point to or clasp his big toe]
This little pig stayed at home [clasp his second toe]
This little pig had roast beef [clasp his third toe]
This little pig had none [clasp his fourth toe]
And this little pig went 'wee wee wee wee' [clasp his little toe and then
    run your fingers all the way up to his chin]
All the way home

Round and round the garden [move your finger round and round on
    the palm of his hand]
Like a teddy bear
One step, two steps [big steps with your fingers creeping up his arm]
Tickly under there [gently tickle under his arm or chin]

Two little dicky birds sitting on a **wall** [start with hands flat; if you
    like, put a strip of paper on the top of both index fingers to make
    them conspicuous]
One named Peter [raise the left index finger and make it dance]
One named Paul [raise the right index finger and make it dance]
Fly away Peter [wave hand behind you and bring out again with index
    finger bent to hide Peter]
Fly away Paul [repeat with other hand]
Come back Peter [wave hand behind you and bring out again with

index finger visible]
Come back Paul [repeat with other hand]

Where is Thumbkin? [to the tune of 'Frère Jacques'; start the song
with hands behind your back, pretending to look for Thumbkin]
Where is Thumbkin?
Here I am! [right hand out with thumb up]
Here I am! [left hand out with thumb up]
How are you today, Sir? [wiggling right thumb as it 'speaks']
Very well, I thank you [wiggling left thumb as it 'answers']
Run away [right hand behind back again]
Run and play [left hand behind back again]

Open, shut them, [open and shut your hands]
Open, shut them,
Give a little clap [clap!]
Open, shut them
Open, shut them,
Lay them in your lap.
Creep them, creep them, [begin creeping]
Creep them, creep them,
Right up to your chin.
Open wide your little mouth [open]
But do not let them in!

Incy Wincy spider
Climbed the water spout [hand and finger movements]
Down came the rain [hand and finger movements]
And washed poor Incy out
Out came the sun [arms up and wide – shining]

And dried up all the rain
So Incy Wincy spider
Climbed up the spout again.

COUNTING SONGS

One, two, three, four, five
Once I caught a fish alive
Six, seven, eight, nine, ten
Then I let him go again.
Why did you let him go?
Because he bit my finger so
Which finger did he bite?
This little finger on the right.

One, two, buckle my shoe,
Three, four, shut the door,
Five, six, pick up sticks,
Seven, eight, lay them straight,
Nine, ten, a big fat hen.

One, two, three, four,
Mary's at the cottage door.
Five, six, seven, eight,
Eating cherries off a plate.

One potato, two potato, three potato, four,
Five potato, six potato, seven potato, more!

Five little ducks went out one day,
Over the hills and far away,
Mother Duck said, 'Quack, quack, quack, quack!'
But only four little ducks came back.

       *   *   *

Four little ducks went out one day . . .
But only three little ducks came back.

       *   *   *

Three little ducks went out one day . . .
But only two little ducks came back.

       *   *   *

Two little ducks went out one day . . .
But only one little ducks came back.

       *   *   *

One little duck went out one day,
Over the hills and far away,
Mother Duck said, 'Quack, quack, quack, quack!'
But none of her five little ducks came back.

       *   *   *

Sad Mother Duck went out one day,
Over the hills and far way,
Mother Duck said, 'Quack, quack, quack, quack!'
And all of her five little ducks came back.

(As you sing this song, use your fingers to make each duck go 'over the hills and far away' and to count the number of ducks left.)

OTHER SONGS YOU MIGHT REMEMBER

A-hunting we will go

Alphabet song

Baa baa black sheep

Dance little baby, dance with me

Diddle diddle dumpling my son John

Ding dong dell

Do you know the muffin man?

Doe, a deer

Down by the station

The farmer in the dell

Fire's burning

The fox

Frère Jacques

Froggie went a-courting

Galumph went the little green frog one day

Here we go looby loo

Here we go round the mulberry bush

Hey diddle diddle the cat and the fiddle

Hickory dickory dock

The Hokey Pokey

Hot cross buns

How much is that doggie in the window

Humpty Dumpty sat on a wall

I had a little nut tree

If you're happy and you know it

I'm a little teapot

It's a small world

It's raining, it's pouring

Jack and Jill

Jamaican farewell

Kiss me, honey, honey, kiss me

Lavender's blue dilly dilly

Little Bo Peep

Little Peter Rabbit had a fly upon his nose

Little Jack Horner

London Bridge is falling down

Lucy Locket lost her pocket

Mary had a little lamb

Mary Mary quite contrary

Michael row the boat ashore

Miss Molly had a dolly

Mr Frog jumped out of the pond one day

Mrs Snail, Mrs Snail

My grandfather's clock

Never smile at a crocodile

Number one (The Wiggles)

Oh Susanna

Oh, the grand old Duke of York, he had ten thousand men

Oh where, oh where has my little dog gone

Old MacDonald had a farm

One, two, three four five

Oranges and lemons

Polly put the kettle on

Polly wolly doodle

Puff the magic dragon

Pussy cat, pussy cat

Rain, rain, go away

Red and yellow and pink and green, purple and orange and blue (I can sing a rainbow)

Row, row, row your boat

Rubber duckie

See how I'm jumping

She'll be coming round the mountain

Sing a song of sixpence

Skip to my loo

Teddy bears' picnic

This old man

Three blind mice

Three little kittens

The wheels on the bus

Yankee Doodle

Zip-a-dee-doo-dah

Further Reading

BOOKS

Beck, Joan, *How to Raise a Brighter Child: The case for early learning*, Souvenir Press, London, 1968

Biddulph, Steve, *The Secret of Happy Children*, HarperCollins, NSW, 1998

Britton, Lesley, *Montessori Play & Learn*, Three Rivers Press (Random House), USA, 1992

Clark, Graeme, *Restoring the Senses*, Boyer Lectures, 2007, <www.abc. net.au/rn/boyerlectures/stories/2007/2084224.htm>

Derham, Frances, *Art for the Child Under Seven*, Australian Preschool Association, Canberra, 1962

Downey, Peter, *So You're Going to be a Dad*, Simon & Schuster, NSW, 2005

Engelmann, Siegfried, & Therese Engelmann, *Give Your Child a Superior Mind*, Simon & Schuster, USA, 1966

Ewing, Robyn (ed.), *Beyond the Reading Wars*, Primary English Teaching Association, NSW, 2006

Fearnley-Whittingstall, Hugh & Fizz Carr, *The River Cottage Family*

Cookbook, Hodder & Stoughton, London, 2005

Fox, Mem, *Reading Magic: Why reading aloud to our children will change their lives forever*, Harcourt, New York, 2001

Friedman, Thomas L., *The World is Flat*, Picador, USA, 2007.

Gladwell, Malcolm, *Outliers: The Story of Success*, Allen Lane, USA, 2008

Goleman, Daniel, *Emotional Intelligence*, Bloomsbury, USA, 1996

Goleman, Daniel, *Social Intelligence*, Bantam, USA, 2007

Gopnik, Alison, Andrew Meltzogg & Patricia Kuhl, *How Babies Think: The science of childhood*, Phoenix (The Orion Publishing Group Ltd), London, 2001

Jennings, Paul, *The Reading Bug . . . and how to help your child catch it*, Puffin Books, Australia, 2004

Kolbe, Ursula, *Rapunzel's Supermarket: All about young children and their art*, Peppinot Press, NSW, 2007

Lawrence, Lynne, *Montessori Read and Write: A parents' guide to literacy for children*, Ebury Press, London, 1998

Montessori, Maria, *The Absorbent Mind*, Holt, Rinehart and Winston, New York, 1967

Rossmanith, Angela, *When Will the Children Play?*, Mandarin, Victoria, 1997

Sachs, Oliver, *Musicophilia: Tales of music and the brain*, Alfred A. Knopf, New York, 2008

Specialist Children's Booksellers, *Don't Leave Childhood Without . . .: A guide to the best books for children*, Nooitgedacht Enterprises, NSW, 2004

Stephenson, Susan, *The Joyful Child: For birth to three years (Michael Olaf's Essential Montessori Series)*, The Michael Olaf Montessori Company, California, 1998

Thomson, Sue, Nicole Wernert, Catherine Underwood & Marina

Nicholas, TIMSS (Trends in International Mathematics and Science Study), 2007: *Taking a Closer Look at Mathematics and Science Study in Australia*, Australian Council for Educational Research (ACER), <www.acer.edu.au/documents/TIMSS_2007-AustraliaFull Report.pdf>

UK House of Commons Education and Skills Committee Report on Teaching Children to Read, Eighth Report of Session 2004–05

WEBSITES

BabyCentre UK <www.babycentre.co.uk>

BBC – CBeebies <www.bbc.co.uk/cbeebies>

Children's Book Council of Australia <www.cbc.org.au>

Chris Cheng, Ambassador of National Literacy and Numeracy Week <www.chrischeng.com/literacyweek.htm>

Early Childhood Australia <www.earlychildhoodaustralia.org.au>

Enchanted Learning – ideas for crafts, games and other activities <www.enchantedlearning.com>

Essential Baby (Fairfax Digital) <www.essentialbaby.com.au>

First School – preschool activities resources and information <www.firstschool.ws>

Kids' Games <www.gameskidsplay.net>

KidsHealth (Nemours Foundation) <www.kidshealth.org>

Kindermusik Australia and New Zealand <www.kindermusik.com.au>

Montessori Australia <www.montessori.org.au>

Nursery Rhymes – lyrics and origins <www.rhymes.org.uk>

Parenting and Babytalk <www.parenting.com>

Raising Children Network – Australian parenting website <www.raisingchildren.net.au>

ACKNOWLEDGEMENTS

We appreciated the many discussions we had with family members, colleagues and friends about this topic and gratefully acknowledge their inspiration, insight and ideas.

We would especially like to thank Jonathan Richards for editorial advice every time we asked, and Nicci Dodanwela, our editor, for her interest in the subject matter and for encouraging and supporting our ideas.

We wish to acknowledge the use of the following quotes:

Bernard Levin (p.39), *If You Want My Opinion*, published by Jonathan Cape, London, 1992; Arundhati Roy (p.47), *The God of Small Things*, published by HarperCollins, London, 1998; Daniel Goleman (p.53), *Emotional Intelligence*, published by Bantam, New York, 1997; Roald Dahl (p.83), *Charlie and the Chocolate Factory*, published by Alfred A. Knopf, 1964, New York; Maria Montessori (p.86), adapted from *The Absorbent Mind* ©1995 by John Chattin-McNichols, reprinted by permission of Henry Holt and Company, LLC, New York; J. K. Rowling (p.88), *Harry Potter and the Philosopher's Stone* © 1997.